Readings in Literary Criticism 16

CRITICS ON HAWTHORNE

Readings in Literary Criticism

CRITICS ON
HAWTHORNE

Readings in Literary Criticism
Edited by Thomas J. Rountree

University of Miami Press
Coral Gables, Florida

Since this page cannot legibly accommodate all of the copyright notices, the pages following constitute an extension of the copyright page.

International Standard Book Number 0-87024-209-1
Library of Congress Catalog Card Number 78-159297
Copyright © 1972 by University of Miami Press
All rights reserved
Printed in the United States of America

Third Printing, 1977

CONTENTS

ACKNOWLEDGMENTS

Richard P. Adams: from *The New England Quarterly*, vol. 30, 1957. Copyright © 1957 by Richard P. Adams. Reprinted by permission of the publisher.

William B. Dillingham: from *Nineteenth-Century Fiction*, vol. 14, no. 1, 1959. Copyright © 1959 by The Regents of the University of California. Reprinted by permission of The Regents.

Charles Feidelson, Jr.: from *Symbolism and American Literature*. Copyright © 1953 by The University of Chicago Press. Reprinted by permission of the publisher.

Richard Harter Fogle: from *Hawthorne's Fiction: The Light and the Dark*. Copyright 1952, 1964 by the University of Oklahoma Press. Reprinted by permission of the publisher.

D. H. Lawrence: from *Studies in Classic American Literature*. Copyright 1923, renewed 1951 by Frieda Lawrence. Reprinted by permission of The Viking Press, Inc.

F. O. Matthiessen: from *American Renaissance*. Copyright 1941 by Oxford University Press, Inc. Reprinted by permission of the publisher.

Peter B. Murray: from *PMLA*, vol. 75, 1960. Copyright © 1960 by the Modern Language Association of America. Reprinted by permission of the publisher.

V. L. Parrington: from *Main Currents in American Thought*, vol. 2. Copyright 1927 by Harcourt Brace Jovanovich, Inc.; renewed 1955 by the author, Louis P. Tucker, and Elizabeth P. Thomas. Reprinted by permission of the publisher.

Donald A. Ringe: from *PMLA*, vol. 65, 1950. Copyright © 1950 by the Modern Language Association of America. Reprinted by permission of the publisher.

Constance Rourke: from *American Humor*. Copyright 1931 by Harcourt Brace Jovanovich, Inc.; renewed 1959 by Alice D. Fore. Reprinted by permission of the publisher.

Robert E. Spiller: from *The Cycle of American Literature*. Copyright © 1955 by Macmillan. Reprinted by permission of the publisher.

Dorothy Waples: from *American Literature*, vol. 13, 1941. Copyright © 1941 by Duke University Press. Reprinted by permission of the publisher.

Yvor Winters: from *In Defense of Reason*. Copyright © 1947 by Yvor Winters. Reprinted by permission of The Swallow Press, Chicago.

INTRODUCTION

EVER SINCE Nathaniel Hawthorne published *The Scarlet Letter* in 1850, some quantity of his writing has been continuously in print right up to the present moment. Much the same can be said of critical reaction to his work.

He did not go entirely unnoticed before the midcentury, however. He had published in numerous periodicals for seven years before he gathered his *Twice-Told Tales* in 1837, and he received comments from both editors and friends. But in the early days his chief public critic was Edgar Allan Poe, who hailed him for his originality in 1842 and then reacted unfavorably five years later.

When in March of 1850 he published *The Scarlet Letter* as his first mature novel (he had anonymously published and hastily recalled *Fanshawe* in 1828), Hawthorne became, in a sense, the literary property of the professional critic as well as of the general reader. While others focused on the new book, Herman Melville masked himself as "a Virginian Spending July in Vermont" and belatedly but enthusiastically reviewed *Mosses from an Old Manse* (1846), discovering therein the significant theme of "blackness" which has fascinated other critics ever since. Curiously enough, *Harper's New Monthly Magazine,* born in June of 1850, did not review *The Scarlet Letter,* but during the next two years it proudly quoted or cited numerous good foreign criticisms of the novelist. Hawthorne's fame was spreading beyond his own country: to the *Athenaeum* in Britain, *Revue des Deux Mondes* in France, *Grenzboten* in Germany.

Between his death in 1864 and the turn of the century, Hawthorne gained a special revered status in American schools; but much of the criticism, while respectful enough still, tended to become patronizing, perhaps because of the rising interest in fictional realism which continued well into the twentieth century and ran counter to moral allegory. One can note the continuity of critical reference to realism, for instance, in the essays by Anthony Trollope and Yvor Winters. One can also sense the patronizing attitude in Leslie Stephen's attempt at historic and geographic "placement" of Hawthorne. And there is perhaps a bit of this attitude in Henry James, who nonetheless recognized Hawthorne's deep psychological aspects and important "historic consciousness."

The year 1950 is probably not quite the watershed in Hawthorne criticism that some have felt it to be, and yet some truth adheres to one writer's statement that earlier critics of the century "strove to recapture Hawthorne's gentle melancholy and antiquarian charm." Many concentrated on the man—his personality and particular genius—and slighted his works. By and large, it *was* after 1950 that the critics began to insist upon and emphasize the works themselves: the symbolism of their image-patterns and the didacticism in their steady moral purpose. Still, James had noted their psychological aspects and

Dorothy Waples had soundly explored implications for Freudianism in one novel prior to so thorough a treatment as Frederick Crews' recent *Sins of the Fathers*. Similarly the treatment of Hawthorne's "meaningful ambiguities," so fruitful for recent criticism, can be traced at least from Winters' qualified and negative references to what he called the novelist's "formula of alternative possibilities" and from F. O. Matthiessen's similar phrase, "device of multiple choice." Thus some of the more recent criticism of Hawthorne has been notable for its thorough enlargement of earlier hints.

At the same time, much has been new, as I hope that this present collection of edited essays will indicate. It has been my object to represent, as fully as the limits of this book will allow, both the variety of critical approaches to Hawthorne's work and the temporal development of that criticism. Most old and new approaches are here in some degree: the biographical, sociological, allegorical, symbolic, archetypal, thematic, formal, historical, mythic, psychological, comparative. The first section of the book presents early reviews in their chronological order, but thereafter the student of temporal critical development can check the dates of the essays and read them in their historical progression. Sections two and three are designed first for the reader who will want to move from the general to the more specific. Thus I have tried to arrange for the beginning student of criticism to have two major procedures available to him, while at the same time I feel that I have included works which the specialist will want to read if they are new to him or will want to re-read if (as most will doubtless be) they are familiar.

Because of the conflict between the page limitations of the book and my desire to be as representatively inclusive as possible of the extensive body of Hawthorne criticism, I have made every effort to keep the essence in tone and content of the full essays herein represented. However, in some instances the reader may want to seek the original printings for valuable critical extensions such as Richard P. Adams' detailed treatment of the psychological implications of the *Provincial Tales* with regard to Freud and Jung. The good reader, of course, will also want to go on to other criticism, while the best reader will do that and then turn back to Hawthorne's stories and romances.

If this book is instrumental to that result for the best reader, then it will have justified itself, I think, in relation to the continuous printing both of Hawthorne's works and of Hawthorne criticism.

University of South Alabama, 1972   THOMAS J. ROUNTREE

TABLE OF IMPORTANT DATES

1804	Born July 4 in Salem, Massachusetts, the second child (there were two daughters) of Nathaniel and Elizabeth Hathorne.
1808	His sea-captain father died of fever in Surinam.
1813	Injured his foot and was confined to the house for two years.
1816-1819	Lived in Raymond, Maine, on Sebago Lake. Enjoyed hunting, fishing, sailing, skating.
1819	Returned to Salem to attend school.
1821-1825	Attended Bowdoin College in Brunswick, Maine. Added the *w* to his name. Became lifelong friend of Franklin Pierce, Horatio Bridge, Jonathan Cilley, and Henry Wadsworth Longfellow.
1825	Graduated from Bowdoin and returned to Salem, where his mother and sisters were again living. Began twelve-year period as a near recluse, devoting himself to reading and writing, with later interspersed trips into New Hampshire and to Niagara Falls and Detroit.
1828	Published his novel *Fanshawe* anonymously but afterwards tried to destroy all copies.
1830	Began publishing stories in the Salem *Gazette*.
1836	Went to Boston and edited *The American Magazine of Useful and Entertaining Knowledge*. Wrote and compiled *Peter Parley's Universal History*. Was helped on both by his sister Elizabeth.
1837	Published *Twice-Told Tales*. Spent a month in Maine at the home of Horatio Bridge.
1838	Traveled to the Berkshires. His friend Jonathan Cilley was killed in a duel.
1839	Became engaged to Sophia Peabody. Received political appointment as weigher and gauger in the Boston Custom House.
1841	Published children's books: *Grandfather's Chair, Famous Old People,* and *Liberty Tree*. In April joined the utopian Brook Farm Community.
1842	Married Sophia Peabody (July 9) and moved to the Old Manse in Concord, Massachusetts, where he came to know Emerson, Thoreau, Ellery Channing, Margaret Fuller, Bronson Alcott, and other Transcendental leaders. Published enlarged edition of *Twice-Told Tales* and another children's book, *Biographical Stories*.
1845	Returned to Salem.
1846	Installed in April as surveyor of the Salem Custom House, his second Democratic party appointment. Published *Mosses from an Old Manse*. Reviewed Melville's *Typee*, calling it "a very remarkable work."
1849	Dismissed in June from the Custom House by the new Whig administration. Began writing *The Scarlet Letter*. His mother died.
1850	Published *The Scarlet Letter*. Moved in May to a red farmhouse near Lenox, Massachusetts, in the Berkshires. Became friend of Herman Melville, who lived near Pittsfield.

1851	Published *The House of the Seven Gables, The Snow-Image and Other Twice-Told Tales,* and *True Stories from History and Biography.* Left Lenox in November for West Newton and then for Concord, where he bought the house he called "The Wayside."
1852	Published *The Blithedale Romance, A Wonder-Book for Girls and Boys,* and *The Life of Franklin Pierce,* a campaign biography.
1853	Published *Tanglewood Tales for Girls and Boys.*
1853-1857	Following appointment by President Pierce, served as U. S. consul at Liverpool, England.
1857-1859	After resigning the consulship, traveled to Italy, where the Hawthornes (with a son and two daughters) and the Robert Brownings became friends and where the oldest child Una nearly died of fever. Lived in Rome and Florence and began writing an Italian romance before returning to England.
1860	Published *The Marble Faun* (entitled *Transformation* in England). Returned to the Wayside in Concord. Began to fail mysteriously and rapidly in health. Was unable to write successfully.
1861-1862	Worked on *Dr. Grimshawe's Secret* and *Septimius Felton* but could not finish either.
1862	Visited Washington, D.C., and the battlefields of northern Virginia.
1863	Published *Our Old Home,* reworked from his English notebooks. Tried to work on *The Dolliver Romance.*
1864	Accompanied by ex-President Pierce on a carriage trip to the White Mountains to restore his health, died en route in his sleep (May 19) at Plymouth, New Hampshire.

Early Reviews

EDGAR ALLAN POE: 1842

THE BOOK [*Twice-Told Tales*] professes to be a collection of *tales*, yet is, in two respects, misnamed. These pieces are now in their third republication, and, of course, are thrice-told. Moreover, they are by no means *all* tales, either in the ordinary or in the legitimate understanding of the term. Many of them are pure essays, for example, "Sights from a Steeple," "Sunday at Home," "Little Annie's Ramble," "A Rill from the Town-Pump," "The Toll-Gatherer's Day," "The Haunted Mind," "The Sister Years," "Snow-Flakes," "Night Sketches," and "Foot-Prints on the Sea-Shore." We mention these matters chiefly on account of their discrepancy with that marked precision and finish by which the body of the work is distinguished.

Of the Essays just named, we must be content to speak in brief. They are each and all beautiful, without being characterised by the polish and adaptation so visible in the tales proper. A painter would at once note their leading or predominant feature, and style it *repose*. There is no attempt at effect. All is quiet, thoughtful, subdued. Yet this repose may exist simultaneously with high originality of thought; and Mr. Hawthorne has demonstrated the fact. At every turn we meet with novel combinations; yet these combinations never surpass the limits of the quiet. We are soothed as we read; and withal is a calm astonishment that ideas so apparently obvious have never occurred or been presented to us before. Herein our author differs materially from Lamb or Hunt or Hazlitt—who, with vivid originality of manner and expression, have less of the true novelty of thought than is generally supposed, and whose originality, at best, has an uneasy and meretricious quaintness, replete with startling effects unfounded in nature, and inducing trains of reflection which lead to no satisfactory result. The Essays of Hawthorne have much of the character of Irving, with more of originality, and less of finish; while, compared with the Spectator, they have a vast superiority at all points. The Spectator, Mr. Irving, and Mr. Hawthorne have in common that tranquil and subdued manner which we have chosen to denominate *repose;* but, in the case of the two former, this repose is attained rather by the absence of novel combination, or of originality, than otherwise, and consists chiefly in the calm, quiet, unostentatious expression of commonplace thoughts, in an unambitious unadulterated Saxon. In them, by strong effort, we are made to conceive the absence of all. In the essays before us the absence of effort is too obvious to be mistaken, and a strong undercurrent of *suggestion* runs continuously beneath the upper stream of the tranquil thesis. In short, these effusions of Mr. Hawthorne are the product of a truly

imaginative intellect, restrained, and in some measure repressed, by fastidiousness of taste, by constitutional melancholy and by indolence.

But it is of his tales that we desire principally to speak. The tale proper,
in our opinion, affords unquestionably the fairest field for the exercise of the
loftiest talent, which can be afforded by the wide domains of mere prose. Were
we bidden to say how the highest genius could be most advantageously
employed for the best display of its own powers, we should answer, without
hesitation—in the composition of a rhymed poem, not to exceed in length what
might be perused in an hour. . . .

Were we called upon however to designate that class of composition which,
next to such a poem as we have suggested, should best fulfil the demands of
high genius—should offer it the most advantageous field of exertion—we
should unhesitatingly speak of the prose tale, as Mr. Hawthorne has here
exemplified it. We allude to the short prose narrative, requiring from a
half-hour to one or two hours in its perusal. The ordinary novel is objectionable, from its length, for reasons already stated in substance. As it cannot be
read at one sitting, it deprives itself, of course, of the immense force derivable
from *totality*. Worldly interests intervening during the pauses of perusal, mod-
ify, annul, or counteract, in a greater or less degree, the impressions of the book.
But simple cessation in reading would, of itself, be sufficient to destroy the true
unity. In the brief tale, however, the author is enabled to carry out the fulness
of his intention, be it what it may. During the hour of perusal the soul of the
reader is at the writer's control. There are no external or extrinsic influences—
resulting from weariness or interruption.

A skilful literary artist has constructed a tale. If wise, he has not fashioned
his thoughts to accommodate his incidents; but having conceived, with deliberate care, a certain unique or single *effect* to be wrought out, he then invents
such incidents—he then combines such events as may best aid him in estab-
lishing this preconceived effect. If his very initial sentence tend not to the
outbringing of this effect, then he has failed in his first step. In the whole
composition there should be no word written, of which the tendency, direct
or indirect, is not to the one pre-established design. And by such means, with
such care and skill, a picture is at length painted which leaves in the mind of
him who contemplates it with a kindred art, a sense of the fullest satisfaction.
The idea of the tale has been presented unblemished, because undisturbed; and
this is an end unattainable by the novel. Undue brevity is just as exceptionable
here as in the poem; but undue length is yet more to be avoided.

We have said that the tale has a point of superiority even over the poem.
In fact, while the *rhythm* of this latter is an essential aid in the development
of the poem's highest idea—the idea of the Beautiful—the artificialities of this
rhythm are an inseparable bar to the development of all points of thought or
expression which have their basis in *Truth*. But Truth is often, and in very
great degree, the aim of the tale. Some of the finest tales are tales of ratiocina-
tion. Thus the field of this species of composition, if not in so elevated a region
on the mountain of Mind, is a table-land of far vaster extent than the domain
of the mere poem. Its products are never so rich, but infinitely more numerous,

and more appreciable by the mass of mankind. The writer of the prose tale, in short, may bring to his theme a vast variety of modes or inflections of thought and expression—(the ratiocinative, for example, the sarcastic or the humorous) which are not only antagonistical to the nature of the poem, but absolutely forbidden by one of its most peculiar and indispensable adjuncts; we allude of course, to rhythm. It may be added, here, *par parenthèse,* that the author who aims at the purely beautiful in a prose tale is laboring at great disadvantage. For Beauty can be better treated in the poem. Not so with terror, or passion, or horror, or a multitude of such other points. And here it will be seen how full of prejudice are the usual animadversions against those *tales of effect* many fine examples of which were found in the earlier numbers of Blackwood. The impressions produced were wrought in a legitimate sphere of action, and constituted a legitimate although sometimes an exaggerated interest. They were relished by every man of genius: although there were found many men of genius who condemned them without just ground. The true critic will but demand that the design intended be accomplished, to the fullest extent, by the means most advantageously applicable.

We have very few American tales of real merit—we may say, indeed, none, with the exception of "The Tales of a Traveller" of Washington Irving, and these "Twice-Told Tales" of Mr. Hawthorne. . . .

Of Mr. Hawthorne's Tales we would say, emphatically, that they belong to the highest region of Art—an Art subservient to genius of a very lofty order. We had supposed, with good reason for so supposing, that he had been thrust into his present position by one of the impudent *cliques* which beset our literature, and whose pretensions it is our full purpose to expose at the earliest opportunity; but we have been most agreeably mistaken. We know of few compositions which the critic can more honestly commend than these "Twice-Told Tales." As Americans, we feel proud of the book.

Mr. Hawthorne's distinctive trait is invention, creation, imagination, originality—a trait which, in the literature of fiction, is positively worth all the rest. But the nature of originality, so far as regards its manifestation in letters, is but imperfectly understood. The inventive or original mind as frequently displays itself in novelty of *tone* as in novelty of matter. Mr. Hawthorne is original at *all* points.

It would be a matter of some difficulty to designate the best of these tales; we repeat that, without exception, they are beautiful. "Wakefield" is remarkable for the skill with which an old idea—a well-known incident—is worked up or discussed. A man of whims conceives the purpose of quitting his wife and residing *incognito,* for twenty years, in her immediate neighborhood. Something of this kind actually happened in London. The force of Mr. Hawthorne's tale lies in the analysis of the motives which must or might have impelled the husband to such folly, in the first instance, with the possible causes of his perseverance. Upon this thesis a sketch of singular power has been constructed.

"The Wedding Knell" is full of the boldest imagination—an imagination fully controlled by taste. The most captious critic could find no flaw in this production.

"The Minister's Black Veil" is a masterly composition of which the sole defect is that to the rabble its exquisite skill will be *caviare*. The *obvious* meaning of this article will be found to smother its insinuated one. The *moral* put into the mouth of the dying minister will be supposed to convey the *true* import of the narrative; and that a crime of dark dye, (having reference to the "young lady") has been committed, is a point which only minds congenial with that of the author will perceive.

"Mr. Higginbotham's Catastrophe" is vividly original and managed most dexterously.

"Dr. Heidegger's Experiment" is exceedingly well imagined, and executed with surpassing ability. The artist breathes in every line of it.

"The White Old Maid" is objectionable, even more than the "Minister's Black Veil," on the score of its mysticism. Even with the thoughtful and analytic, there will be much trouble in penetrating its entire import.

"The Hollow of the Three Hills" we would quote in full, had we space;— not as evincing higher talent than any of the other pieces, but as affording an excellent example of the author's peculiar ability. The subject is commonplace. A witch subjects the Distant and the Past to the view of a mourner. It has been the fashion to describe, in such cases, a mirror in which the images of the absent appear; or a cloud of smoke is made to arise, and thence the figures are gradually unfolded. Mr. Hawthorne has wonderfully heightened his effect by making the ear, in place of the eye, the medium by which the fantasy is conveyed. The head of the mourner is enveloped in the cloak of the witch, and within its magic folds there arise sounds which have an all-sufficient intelligence. Throughout this article also, the artist is conspicuous—not more in positive than in negative merits. Not only is all done that should be done, but (what perhaps is an end with more difficulty attained) there is nothing done which should not be. Every word *tells*, and there is not a word which does *not* tell. . . .

In the way of objection we have scarcely a word to say of these tales. There is, perhaps, a somewhat too general or prevalent *tone*—a tone of melancholy and mysticism. The subjects are insufficiently varied. There is not so much of *versatility* evinced as we might well be warranted in expecting from the high powers of Mr. Hawthorne. But beyond these trivial exceptions we have really none to make. The style is purity itself. Force abounds. High imagination gleams from every page. Mr. Hawthorne is a man of the truest genius. We only regret that the limits of our Magazine will not permit us to pay him that full tribute of commendation, which, under other circumstances, we should be so eager to pay.

From *Graham's Magazine* (Philadelphia), 20 (May 1842), 298-300.

HERMAN MELVILLE: 1850

IT IS curious how a man may travel along a country road, and yet miss the grandest or sweetest of prospects by reason of an intervening hedge, so like all other hedges, as in no way to hint of the wide landscape beyond. So has it been with me concerning the enchanting landscape in the soul of this Hawthorne, this most excellent Man of Mosses. His "Old Manse" [*Mosses from an Old Manse*] has been written now four years, but I never read it till a day or two since. . . . It may be, however, that all this while the book . . . was only improving in flavor and body. At any rate, it so chanced that this long procrastination eventuated in a happy result. . . .

The sketch of "The Old Apple-Dealer" is conceived in the subtlest spirit of sadness; he whose "subdued and nerveless boyhood prefigured his abortive prime, which, likewise, contained within itself the prophecy and image of his lean and torpid age." Such touches as are in this piece cannot proceed from any common heart. They argue such a depth of tenderness, such a boundless sympathy with all forms of being, such an omnipresent love, that we must needs say that this Hawthorne is here almost alone in his generation,—at least, in the artistic manifestation of these things. Still more. Such touches as these,— and many, very many similar ones, all through his chapters—furnish clues whereby we enter a little way into the intricate, profound heart where they originated. And we see that suffering, some time or other and in some shape or other,—this only can enable any man to depict it in others. All over him, Hawthorne's melancholy rests like an Indian-summer, which, though bathing a whole country in one softness, still reveals the distinctive hue of every towering hill and each far-winding vale.

But it is the least part of genius that attracts admiration. Where Hawthorne is known, he seems to be deemed a pleasant writer, with a pleasant style,—a sequestered, harmless man, from whom any deep and weighty thing would hardly be anticipated—a man who means no meanings. But there is no man, in whom humor and love, like mountain peaks, soar to such a rapt height as to receive the irradiations of the upper skies;—there is no man in whom humor and love are developed in that high form called genius; no such man can exist without also possessing, as the indispensable complement of these, a great, deep intellect, which drops down into the universe like a plummet. Or, love and humor are only the eyes through which such an intellect views this world. The great beauty in such a mind is but the product of its strength. What, to all readers, can be more charming than the piece entitled "Monsieur du Miroir;"

and to a reader at all capable of fully fathoming it, what, at the same time, can possess more mystical depth of meaning?—yes, there he sits and looks at me,—this "shape of mystery," this "identical Monsieur du Miroir." "Methinks I should tremble now, were his wizard power of gliding through all impediments in search of me, to place him suddenly before my eyes." . . .

"The Christmas Banquet," and "The Bosom Serpent," would be fine subjects for a curious and elaborate analysis, touching the conjectural parts of the mind that produced them. For spite of all the Indian-summer sunlight on the hither side of Hawthorne's soul, the other side—like the dark half of the physical sphere—is shrouded in a blackness, ten times black. But this darkness but gives more effect to the ever-moving dawn, that for ever advances through it, and circumnavigates his world. Whether Hawthorne has simply availed himself of this mystical blackness as a means to the wondrous effects he makes it to produce in his lights and shades; or whether there really lurks in him, perhaps unknown to himself, a touch of Puritanic gloom,—this, I cannot altogether tell. Certain it is, however, that this great power of blackness in him derives its force from its appeals to that Calvinistic sense of Innate Depravity and Original Sin, from whose visitations, in some shape or other, no deeply thinking mind is always and wholly free. For, in certain moods, no man can weigh this world without throwing in something, somehow like Original Sin, to strike the uneven balance. At all events, perhaps no writer has ever wielded this terrific thought with greater terror than this same harmless Hawthorne. Still more: this black conceit pervades him through and through. You may be witched by his sunlight,—transported by the bright gildings in the skies he builds over you; but there is the blackness of darkness beyond; and even his bright gildings but fringe and play upon the edges of thunder-clouds. In one word, the world is mistaken in this Nathaniel Hawthorne. He himself must often have smiled at its absurd misconception of him. He is immeasurably deeper than the plummet of the mere critic. For it is not the brain that can test such a man; it is only the heart. You cannot come to know greatness by inspecting it; there is no glimpse to be caught of it, except by intuition; you need not ring it, you but touch it, and you find it is gold.

Now, it is that blackness in Hawthorne, of which I have spoken, that so fixes and fascinates me. It may be, nevertheless, that it is too largely developed in him. Perhaps he does not give us a ray of his light for every shade of his dark. But however this may be, this blackness it is that furnishes the infinite obscure of his back-ground,—that back-ground, against which Shakspeare plays his grandest conceits, the things that have made for Shakspeare his loftiest but most circumscribed renown, as the profoundest of thinkers. . . .

But if this view of the all-popular Shakspeare be seldom taken by his readers, and if very few who extol him have ever read him deeply, or, perhaps, only have seen him on the tricky stage (which alone made, and is still making him his mere mob renown)—if few men have time, or patience, or palate, for the spiritual truth as it is in that great genius;—it is then no matter of surprise, that in a contemporaneous age, Nathaniel Hawthorne is a man as yet almost utterly mistaken among men. Here and there, in some quiet armchair in the noisy town, or some deep nook among the noiseless mountains, he may be appreciated for something of what he is. But unlike Shakspeare, who was forced to the contrary course by circumstances, Hawthorne (either from simple disinclination, or else from inaptitude) refrains from all the popularizing noise and show of broad farce and blood-besmeared tragedy; content with the still, rich utterance of a great intellect in repose, and which sends few thoughts into circulation, except they be arterialized at his large warm lungs, and expanded in his honest heart.

Nor need you fix upon that blackness in him, if it suit you not. Nor, indeed, will all readers discern it; for it is, mostly, insinuated to those who may best understand it, and account for it; it is not obtruded upon everyone alike.

Some may start to read of Shakspeare and Hawthorne on the same page. They may say, that if an illustration were needed, a lesser light might have sufficed to elucidate this Hawthorne, this small man of yesterday. But I am not willingly one of those who, as touching Shakspeare at least, exemplify the maxim of Rochefoucault, that "we exalt the reputation of some, in order to depress that of others;"—who, to teach all noble-souled aspirants that there is no hope for them, pronounce Shakspeare absolutely unapproachable. . . . You must believe in Shakspeare's unapproachability, or quit the country. But what sort of a belief is this for an American, a man who is bound to carry republican progressiveness into Literature as well as into Life? Believe me, my friends, that men, not very much inferior to Shakspeare, are this day being born on the banks of the Ohio. . . .

Now I do not say that Nathaniel of Salem is a greater than William of Avon, or as great. But the difference between the two men is by no means immeasurable. Not a very great deal more, and Nathaniel were verily William. . . .

In treating of Hawthorne, or rather of Hawthorne in his writings (for I never saw the man; and in the chances of a quiet plantation life, remote from his haunts, perhaps never shall); in treating of his works, I say, I have thus far omitted all mention of his "Twice Told Tales," and "Scarlet Letter." Both are excellent, but full of such manifold, strange, and diffusive beauties, that time would all but fail me to point the half of them out. But there are things in those two books, which, had they been written in England a century ago, Nathaniel Hawthorne had utterly displaced many of the bright names we now revere on authority. But I am content to leave Hawthorne to himself, and to the infallible finding of posterity; and however great may be the praise I have bestowed upon him, I feel that in so doing I have more served and honored myself, than him. For, at bottom, great excellence is praise enough to itself; but the feeling of a sincere and appreciative love and admiration towards it, this is relieved by utterance; and warm, honest praise, ever leaves a pleasant flavor in the mouth; and it is an honorable thing to confess to what is honorable in others. . . .

When I yesterday wrote, I had not at all read two particular pieces, to which I now desire to call special attention,—"A Select Party," and "Young Goodman Brown." Here, be it said to all those whom this poor fugitive scrawl of mine may tempt to the perusal of the "Mosses," that they must on no account suffer themselves to be trifled with, disappointed, or deceived by the triviality of many of the titles to these sketches. For in more than one instance, the title utterly belies the piece. It is as if rustic demijohns containing the very best and costliest of Falernian and Tokay, were labeled "Cider," "Perry," and "Elder-berry wine." The truth seems to be, that like many other geniuses, this Man of Mosses takes great delight in hoodwinking the world,—at least, with respect to himself. Personally, I doubt not that he rather prefers to be generally esteemed but a so-so sort of author; being willing to reserve the thorough and acute appreciation of what he is, to that party most qualified to judge—that is, to himself. . . .

But with whatever motive, playful or profound, Nathaniel Hawthorne has chosen to entitle his pieces in the manner he has, it is certain that some of them are directly calculated to deceive—egregiously deceive, the superficial skimmer of pages. . . . You would of course suppose that it ["Young Goodman Brown"] was a simple little tale. . . . Whereas, it is deep as Dante; nor can you finish it, without addressing the author in his own words—"It is yours to penetrate, in every bosom, the deep mystery of sin." . . .

Now this same piece . . . is one of the two that I had not all read yesterday; and I allude to it now, because it is, in itself, such a strong positive illustration of that blackness in Hawthorne, which I had assumed from the mere occasional shadows of it, as revealed in several of the other sketches. But had I previously perused "Young Goodman Brown," I should have been at no pains to draw the conclusion, which I came to at a time when I was ignorant that the book contained one such direct and unqualified manifestation of it. . . .

Gainsay it who will, as I now write, I am Posterity speaking by proxy—and after times will make it more than good, when I declare, that the American, who up to the present day has evinced, in literature, the largest brain with the largest heart, that man is Nathaniel Hawthorne. Moreover, that whatever Nathaniel Hawthorne may hereafter write, "The Mosses from an Old Manse" will be ultimately accounted his master-piece. For there is a sure, though a secret sign in some works which proves the culmination of the powers (only the developable ones, however) that produced them. But I am by no means desirous of the glory of a prophet. I pray Heaven that Hawthorne may *yet* prove me an impostor in this prediction. . . .

From *The Literary World; A Journal of Science, Literature, and Art* (New York), 17 Aug. 1850, pp. 125-27; 24 Aug. 1850, pp. 145-47.

HENRY CHORLEY (?): 1850

THIS [*The Scarlet Letter*] is a most powerful but painful story. Mr. Hawthorne must be well known to our readers as a favourite with the *Athenaeum*. We rate him as among the most original and peculiar writers of American fiction. There is in his works a mixture of Puritan reserve and wild imagination, of passion and description, of the allegorical and the real, which some will fail to understand, and which others will positively reject,—but which, to ourselves, is fascinating, and which entitles him to be placed on a level with Brockden Brown and the author of 'Rip Van Winkle.' 'The Scarlet Letter' will increase his reputation with all who do not shrink from the invention of the tale; but this, as we have said, is more than ordinarily painful. When we have announced that the three characters are a guilty wife, openly punished for her guilt,—her tempter, whom she refuses to unmask, and who during the entire story carries a fair front and an unblemished name among his congregation,—and her husband, who, returning from a long absence at the moment of her sentence, sits himself down betwixt the two in the midst of a small and severe community to work out his slow vengeance on both under the pretext of magnanimous forgiveness,—when we have explained that 'The Scarlet Letter' is the badge of Hester Prynne's shame, we ought to add that we recollect no tale dealing with crime so sad and revenge so subtly diabolical, that is at the same time so clear of fever and of prurient excitement. The misery of the woman is as present in every page as the heading which in the title of the romance symbolizes her punishment. Her terrors concerning her strange elvish child present retribution in a form which is new and natural:—her slow and painful purification through repentance is crowned by no perfect happiness, such as awaits the decline of those who have no dark and bitter past to remember. Then, the gradual corrosion of heart of Dimmesdale, the faithless priest, under the insidious care of the husband, (whose relationship to Hester is a secret known only to themselves,) is appalling; and his final confession and expiation are merely a relief, not a reconciliation.—We are by no means satisfied that passions and tragedies like these are the legitimate subjects for fiction. . . . But if Sin and Sorrow in their most fearful forms are to be presented in any work of art, they have rarely been treated with a loftier severity, purity, and sympathy than in Mr. Hawthorne's 'Scarlet Letter.' The touch of the fantastic befitting a period of society in which ignorant and excitable human creatures conceived each other and themselves to be under the direct "rule and governance" of the Wicked One, is most skilfully administered. The supernatural here never becomes grossly palpable:—the thrill is all the deeper for its action being indefinite, and its source vague and distant.

From *The Athenaeum: Journal of Literature, Science, and the Fine Arts* (London), 15 June 1850, p. 634.

HARPER'S NEW MONTHLY MAGAZINE: 1851

TICKNOR, REED, and Fields have issued *The House of the Seven Gables,* a Romance, by Nathaniel Hawthorne, which is strongly marked with the bold and unique characteristics that have given its author such a brilliant position among American novelists. The scene, which is laid in the old Puritanic town of Salem, extends from the period of the witchcraft excitement to the present time, connecting the legends of the ancient superstition with the recent marvels of animal magnetism, and affording full scope for the indulgence of the most weird and sombre fancies. Destitute of the high-wrought manifestations of passion which distinguished the "Scarlet Letter," it is more terrific in its conception, and not less intense in its execution, but exquisitely relieved by charming portraitures of character, and quaint and comic descriptions of social eccentricities. A deep vein of reflection underlies the whole narrative, often rising naturally to the surface, and revealing the strength of the foundation on which the subtle, aerial inventions of the author are erected. His frequent dashes of humor gracefully blend with the monotone of the story, and soften the harsher colors in which he delights to clothe his portentous conceptions. In no former production of his pen, are his unrivalled powers of description displayed to better advantage. The rusty wooden house in Pyncheon street, with its seven sharp-pointed gables, and its huge clustered chimney—the old elm tree before the door—the grassy yard seen through the lattice-fence, with its enormous fertility of burdocks—and the green moss on the slopes of the roof, with the flowers growing aloft in the air in the nook between two of the gables—present a picture to the eye as distinct as if our childhood had been passed in the shadow of the old weather-beaten edifice. Nor are the characters of the story drawn with less sharp and vigorous perspective. They stand out from the canvas as living realities. In spite of the supernatural drapery in which they are enveloped, they have such a genuine expression of flesh and blood, that we can not doubt we have known them all our days. They have the air of old acquaintance—only we wonder how the artist got them to sit for their likenesses. The grouping of these persons is managed with admirable artistic skill. Old Maid Pyncheon, concealing under her verjuice scowl the unutterable tenderness of a sister—her woman-hearted brother, on whose sensitive nature had fallen such a strange blight—sweet and beautiful Phebe, the noble village-maiden, whose presence is always like that of some shining angel—the dreamy, romantic descendant of the legendary wizard—the bold, bad man of the world, reproduced at intervals in the bloody Colonel, and the unscrupulous Judge—

wise old Uncle Venner—and inappeasable Ned Higgins—are all made to occupy the place on the canvas which shows the lights and shades of their character in the most impressive contrast, and contributes to the wonderful vividness and harmony of the grand historical picture. On the whole, we regard "The House of the Seven Gables," though it exhibits no single scenes that may not be matched in depth and pathos by some of Mr. Hawthorne's previous creations, as unsurpassed by any thing he has yet written, in exquisite beauty of finish, in the skillful blending of the tragic and comic, and in the singular life-like reality with which the wildest traditions of the Puritanic age are combined with the every-day incidents of modern society.

From *Harper's New Monthly Magazine* (New York), 2 (May 1851), 855-56.

LESLIE STEPHEN: 1872

LET US try to determine some of the peculiarities to which Hawthorne owes this strange power of bringing poetry out of the most unpromising materials.

In the first place, then, he had the good fortune to be born in the most prosaic of all countries—the most prosaic, that is, in external appearance, and even in the superficial character of its inhabitants. Hawthorne himself reckoned this as an advantage, though in a very different sense from that in which we are speaking. It was as a patriot, and not as an artist, that he congratulated himself on his American origin. There is a humorous struggle between his sense of the rawness and ugliness of his native land and the dogged patriotism befitting a descendant of the genuine New England Puritans. Hawthorne the novelist writhes at the discords which torture his delicate sensibilities at every step; but instantly Hawthorne the Yankee protests that the very faults are symptomatic of excellence. . . . To my thinking, there is something almost pathetic in this loyal self-deception; and therefore I have never been offended by certain passages in *Our Old Home* which appear to have caused some irritation in touchy Englishmen. There is something, he says by way of apology, which causes an American in England to take up an attitude of antagonism. "These people think so loftily of themselves, and so contemptuously of everybody else, that it requires more generosity than I possess to keep always in perfectly good-humour with them." That may be true; for, indeed, I believe that deep down in the bosom of every Briton, beneath all superficial roots of cosmopolitan philanthropy, there lies an ineradicable conviction that no foreigner is his equal; and to a man of Hawthorne's delicate perceptions, the presence of that sentiment would reveal itself through the most careful disguises. But that which really caused him to cherish his antagonism was, I suspect, something else: he was afraid of loving us too well; he feared to be tempted into a denial of some point of his patriotic creed. . . .

But the problem recurs . . . whether Hawthorne would not have developed into a still greater artist if he had been more richly supplied with the diet [of cultivated and romantic association] so dear to his inmost soul? . . . Hawthorne, if his life had passed where the plough may turn up an antiquity in every furrow, and the whole face of the country is enamelled with ancient culture, might have wrought more gorgeous hues into his tissues, but he might have succumbed to the temptation of producing mere upholstery. The fairy land for which he longed is full of dangerous enchantments, and there are many who have lost in it the vigour which comes from breathing the keen air of every-day life. From that risk Hawthorne was effectually preserved in his New England home. Having to abandon the poetry which is manufactured out of mere external circumstances, he was forced to draw it from deeper sources. With easier means at hand of enriching his pages, he might have left the mine unworked. It is often good for us to have to make bricks without straw. Hawthorne, who was conscious of the extreme difficulty of the problem, and but partially conscious of the success of his solution of it, naturally complained of the severe discipline to which he owed his strength. We who enjoy the results may feel how much he owed to the very sternness of his education and the niggard hand with which his imaginative sustenance was dealt out to him. . . .

The story which perhaps generally passes for his masterpiece is *Transformation* [i.e., *The Marble Faun*], for most readers assume that a writer's longest book must necessarily be his best. In the present case, I think that this method, which has its conveniences, has not led to a perfectly just conclusion. In *Transformation,* Hawthorne has for once the advantage of placing his characters in a land where "a sort of poetic or fairy precinct," as he calls it, is naturally provided for them. The very stones of the streets are full of romance, and he cannot mention a name that has not a musical ring. Hawthorne, moreover, shows his usual tact in confining his aims to the possible. He does not attempt to paint Italian life and manners; his actors belong by birth, or by a kind of naturaliza- tion, to the colony of the American artists in Rome; and he therefore does not labour under the difficulty of being in imperfect sympathy with his creatures. Rome is a mere background, and surely a most felicitous background, to the little group of persons who are effectually detached from all such vulgarizing associations with the mechanism of daily life in less poetical countries. . . . But without cavilling at what is indisputably charming, and without dwelling upon certain defects of construction which slightly mar the general beauty of the story, it has another weakness which it is impossible quite to overlook. . . . There are, to put it bluntly, passages which strike us like masses of undigested guide-book. . . .

There is almost a superabundance of minute local colour in his American romances, as, for example, in the *House of the Seven Gables;* but still, every touch, however minute, is steeped in the sentiment and contributes to the general effect. . . . A human soul, even in America, is more interesting to us than all the churches and picture-galleries in the world; and, therefore, it is as well that Hawthorne should not be tempted to the too easy method of putting fine description in place of sentiment. . . .

His idealism does not consist in conferring grandeur upon vulgar objects by tinging them with the reflection of deep emotion. He rather shrinks than otherwise from describing the strongest passions, or shows their working by indirect touches and under a side-light. An excellent example of his peculiar method occurs in what is in some respects the most perfect of his works, the *Scarlet Letter.* There, again, we have the spectacle of a man tortured by a life-long repentance. The Puritan clergyman . . . yields under terrible pressure to the temptation of escaping from the scene of his prolonged torture with the partner of his guilt. And then, as he is returning homewards after yielding a reluctant consent to the flight, we are invited to contemplate the agony of his soul. The form which it takes is curiously characteristic. No vehement pangs of remorse, or desperate hopes of escape, overpower his faculties in any simple and straightforward fashion. The poor minister is seized with a strange hallucination. He meets a venerable deacon, and can scarcely restrain himself from uttering blasphemies about the communion-supper. . . . And, finally, he longs to greet a rough sailor with a "volley of good round, solid, satisfactory, and heaven-defying oaths." The minister, in short, is in that state of mind which gives birth in its victim to a belief in diabolical possession; and the meaning is pointed by an encounter with an old lady, who, in the popular belief, was one of Satan's miserable slaves and dupes, the witches, and is said—for Hawthorne never introduces the supernatural without toning it down by a supposed legendary transmission—to have invited him to meet her at the blasphemous sabbath in the forest. The sin of endeavouring to escape from the punishment of his sins had brought him into sympathy with wicked mortals and perverted spirits.

This mode of setting forth the agony of a pure mind, tainted by one irremovable blot, is undoubtedly impressive to the imagination in a high degree; far more impressive, we may safely say, than any quantity of such rant as very inferior writers could have poured out with the utmost facility on such an occasion. Yet I am inclined to think that a poet of the highest order would have produced the effect by more direct means. Remorse overpowering and absorbing does not embody itself in these recondite and, one may almost say, over-ingenious fancies. Hawthorne does not give us so much the pure passion as some of its collateral effects. He is still more interested in the curious psychological problem than moved by sympathy with the torture of the soul.

. . .

Every pure Yankee represents one or both of two types—the descendant of the Puritans and the shrewd peddler. . . . In Hawthorne it would seem that the peddling element had been reduced to its lowest point; the more spiritual element had been refined till it is probable enough that the ancestral shadow would have refused to recognize the connection. The old dogmatical framework to which he attached such vast importance had dropped out of his descendant's mind, and had been replaced by dreamy speculation, obeying no laws save those imposed by its own sense of artistic propriety. But we may often recognize, even where we cannot express in words, the strange family likeness which exists in characteristics which are superficially antagonistic. The man of action may be bound by subtle ties to the speculative metaphysician; and Hawthorne's mind, amidst the most obvious differences, had still an affinity to his remote forefathers. Their bugbears had become his playthings; but the witches, though they have no reality, have still a fascination for him. The interest which he feels in them, even in their now shadowy state, is a proof that he would have believed in them in good earnest a century and a half earlier. The imagination, working in a different intellectual atmosphere, is unable to project its images upon the external world; but it still forms them in the old shape. His solitary musings necessarily employ a modern dialect, but they often turn on the topics which occurred to Jonathan Edwards in the woods of Conne, Instead of the old Puritan speculations about predestination and freewi dwells upon the transmission by natural laws of an hereditary curse, and the strange blending of good and evil, which may cause sin to be an awake... impulse in a human soul. . . . He loves the marvellous, not in the vulgar sense of the word, but as a symbol of the perplexity which encounters every thoughtful man in his journey through life. Similar tenets as an earlier period might, with almost equal probability, have led him to the stake as a dabbler in forbidden sciences, or have caused him to be revered as one to whom a deep spiritual instinct had been granted.

Meanwhile, as it was his calling to tell stories to readers of the English language in the nineteenth century, his power is exercised in a different sphere. No modern writer has the same skill in so using the marvellous as to interest without unduly exciting our incredulity. He makes, indeed, no positive demands on our credulity. The strange influences which are suggested rather than obtruded upon us, are kept in the background so as not to invite, nor, indeed, to render possible the application of scientific tests. . . . His ghosts are confined to their proper sphere, the twilight of the mind, and never venture into the broad glare of daylight. We can see them so long as we do not gaze directly at them; when we turn to examine them they are gone, and we are left in doubt whether they were realities or an ocular delusion generated in our fancy by some accidental collocation of half-seen objects. So in the *House of the Seven Gables* we may hold what opinion we please as to the reality of the curse which hangs over the family of the Pyncheons and the strange connection between them and their hereditary antagonists; in the *Scarlet Letter* we may, if we like, hold that there was really more truth in the witch legends which colour the imaginations of the actors than we are apt to dream of in our philosophy; and in *Transformation* we are left finally in doubt as to the great question of Donatello's ears, and the mysterious influence which he retains over the animal world so long as he is unstained by bloodshed. . . .

In fact Hawthorne was able to tread in that magic circle [of the marvelous] only by an exquisite refinement of taste, and by a delicate sense of humour, which is the best preservative against all extravagance. Both qualities combine in that tender delineation of character which is, after all, one of his greatest charms. His Puritan blood shows itself in sympathy, not with the stern side of the ancestral creed, but with the feebler characters upon whom it weighed as an oppressive terror. He resembles, in some degree, poor Clifford Pyncheon, whose love of the beautiful makes him suffer under the stronger will of his relatives and the prim stiffness of their home. He exhibits the suffering of such a character all the more effectively because with his kindly compassion, there is mixed a delicate flavour of irony. . . .

From *The Cornhill Magazine* (London), 26 (December 1872), 717-34.

ANTHONY TROLLOPE: 1879

THERE NEVER surely was a powerful, active, continually effective mind less round, more lop-sided, than that of Nathaniel Hawthorne. If there were aught of dispraise in this, it would not be said by me,—by an Englishman of an American whom I knew, by an Englishman of letters of a brother on the other side of the water, much less by me, an English novelist, of an American novelist. . . . [From] Hawthorne we could not have obtained that weird, mysterious, thrilling charm with which he has awed and delighted us had he not allowed his mind to revel in one direction, so as to lose its fair proportions.

I have been specially driven to think of this by the strong divergence between Hawthorne and myself. It has always been my object to draw my little pictures as like to life as possible. . . . Hawthorne, on the other hand, has dealt with persons and incidents which were often but barely within the bounds of possibility,—which were sometimes altogether without those bounds,—and has determined that his readers should be carried out of their own little mundane ways, and brought into a world of imagination in which their intelligence might be raised, if only for a time, to something higher than the common needs of common life.

That some remnant of Puritan asceticism should be found in the writings of a novelist from Concord, in Massachusetts, would seem natural to an English reader,—though I doubt whether there be much of the flavor of the Mayflower left at present to pervade the literary parterres of Boston. But, had that been the Hawthorne flavor, readers both in England and in the States would have accepted it without surprise.

It is, however, altogether different, though ascetic enough. The predominating quality of Puritan life was hard, good sense,—a good sense which could value the realities of life while it rejected the frivolities,—a good sense to which buttered cakes, water-tight boots, and a pretty wife, or a kind husband could endear themselves. Hawthorne is severe, but his severity is never of a nature to form laws for life. His is a mixture of romance and austerity, quite as far removed from the realities of Puritanism as it is from the sentimentalism of poetry. He creates a melancholy which amounts almost to remorse in the minds of his readers. There falls upon them a conviction of some unutterable woe. . . . You are beyond measure depressed by the weird tale that is told to you, but you become conscious of a certain grandness of nature in being susceptible of such suffering. . . . You have been ennobled by that familiarity with sorrow. You have been, as it were, sent through the fire and purged of so much of your dross. . . . He will have plunged you into melancholy, he will have overshadowed you with black forebodings, he will almost have crushed you with imaginary sorrows; but he will have enabled you to feel yourself an inch taller during the process. Something of the sublimity of the transcendent, something of the mystery of the unfathomable, something of the brightness of the celestial, will have attached itself to you, and you will all but think that you too might live to be sublime, and revel in mingled light and mystery.

The creations of American literature generally are no doubt more given to the speculative,—less given to the realistic,— than are those of English literature. . . . But in no American writer is to be found the same predominance of weird imagination as in Hawthorne. There was something of it in M. G. Lewis—our Monk Lewis as he came to be called, from the name of a tale which he wrote; but with him, as with many others, we feel that they have been weird because they have desired to be so. They have struggled to achieve the tone with which their works are pervaded. With Hawthorne we are made to think that he could not have been anything else if he would. It is as though he could certainly have been nothing else in his own inner life. We know that such was not actually the case. Though a man singularly reticent,—what we generally call shy,—he could, when things went well with him, be argumentative, social, and cheery. . . . And yet his imagination was such that the creations of his brain could not have been other than such as I have described. . . .

"The Scarlet Letter" is, on the English side of the water, perhaps the best known. It is so terrible in its pictures of diseased human nature as to produce most questionable delight. The reader's interest never flags for a moment. There is nothing of episode or digression. The author is always telling his one story with a concentration of energy which, as we can understand, must have made it impossible for him to deviate. The reader will certainly go on with it to the end very quickly, entranced, excited, shuddering, and at times almost wretched. His consolation will be that he too has been able to see into these black deeps of the human heart. The story is one of jealousy,—of love and jealousy,—in which love is allowed but little scope, but full play is given to the hatred which can spring from injured love. . . .

The personages in it with whom the reader will interest himself are four,— the husband, the minister who has been the sinful lover, the woman, and the child. The reader is expected to sympathize only with the woman,—and will sympathize only with her. The husband, an old man who has knowingly married a young woman who did not love him, is a personification of that feeling of injury which is supposed to fall upon a man when his honor has been stained by the falseness of a wife. He has left her and has wandered away, not even telling her of his whereabout. He comes back to her without a sign. The author tells us that he had looked to find his happiness in her solicitude and care for him. The reader, however, gives him credit for no love. But the woman was his wife, and he comes back and finds that she had gone astray. Her he despises, and is content to leave to the ascetic cruelty of the town magistrates; but to find the man out and bring the man to his grave by slow torture is enough of employment for what is left to him of life and energy.

With the man, the minister, the lover, the reader finds that he can have nothing in common, though he is compelled to pity his sufferings. The woman has held her peace when she was discovered and reviled and exposed. She will never whisper his name, never call on him for any comfort or support in her misery; but he, though the very shame is eating into his soul, lives through the seven years of the story, a witness of her misery and solitude, while he himself is surrounded by the very glory of sanctity. Of the two, indeed, he is the greater sufferer. While shame only deals with her, conscience is at work with him. But there can be no sympathy, because he looks on and holds his peace. Her child says to him,—her child, not knowing that he is her father, not knowing what she says, but in answer to him when he would fain take her little hand in his during the darkness of night,—"Wilt thou stand here with mother and me to-morrow noontide"? He can not bring himself to do that, though he struggles hard to do it, and therefore we despise him. He can not do it till the hand of death is upon him, and then the time is too late for reparation in the reader's judgment. Could we have sympathized with a pair of lovers, the human element would have prevailed too strongly for the author's purpose.

He seems hardly to have wished that we should sympathize even with her; or, at any rate, he has not bid us in so many words to do so, as is common with authors. Of course, he has wished it. He has intended that the reader's heart should run over with ruth for the undeserved fate of that wretched woman. And it does. She is pure as undriven snow. We know that at some time far back she loved and sinned, but it was done when we did not know her. We are not told so, but come to understand, by the wonderful power of the writer in conveying that which he never tells, that there has been no taint of foulness in her love, though there has been deep sin. He never even tells us why that letter A has been used, though the abominable word is burning in our ears from first to last. We merely see her with her child, bearing her lot with patience, seeking for no comfort, doing what good she can in her humble solitude by the work of her hands, pointed at from all by the finger of scorn, but the purest, the cleanest, the fairest also among women. She never dreams of supposing that she ought not to be regarded as vile, while the reader's heart glows with a longing to take her soft hand and lead her into some pleasant place where the world shall be pleasant and honest and kind to her. I can fancy a reader so loving the image of Hester Prynne as to find himself on the verge of treachery to the real Hester of flesh and blood who may have a claim upon him. Sympathy can not go beyond that; and yet the author deals with her in a spirit of assumed hardness, almost as though he assented to the judgment and the manner in which it was carried out. In this, however, there is a streak of that satire with which Hawthorne always speaks of the peculiar institutions of his own country. The worthy magistrates of Massachusetts are under his lash throughout the story, and so is the virtue of her citizens and the chastity of her matrons, which can take delight in the open shame of a woman whose sin has been discovered. Indeed, there is never a page written by Hawthorne not tinged by satire.

The fourth character is that of the child, Pearl. Here the author has, I think, given way to a temptation, and in doing so has not increased the power of his story. The temptation was, that Pearl should add a picturesque element by being an elf and also a charming child. Elf she is, but, being so, is incongruous with all else in the story, in which, unhuman as it is, there is nothing of the ghost-like, nothing of the unnatural. The old man becomes a fiend, so to say, during the process of the tale; but he is a man-fiend. And Hester becomes sublimated almost to divine purity; but she is still simply a woman. The minister is tortured beyond the power of human endurance; but neither do his sufferings nor his failure of strength adequate to support them come to him from any miraculous agency. But Pearl is miraculous,—speaking, acting, and thinking like an elf,—and is therefore, I think, a drawback rather than an aid. The desolation of the woman, too, would have been more perfect without the child. It seems as though the author's heart had not been hard enough to make her live alone. . . .

Hatred, fear, and shame are the passions which revel through the book. To show how a man may so hate as to be content to sacrifice everything to his hatred; how another may fear so that, even though it be for the rescue of his soul, he can not bring himself to face the reproaches of the world; how a woman may bear her load of infamy openly before the eyes of all men,—this has been Hawthorne's object. And surely no author was ever more successful. The relentless purpose of the man, in which is exhibited no passion, in which there is hardly a touch of anger, is as fixed as the hand of Fate. No one in the town knew that the woman was his wife. She had never loved him. He had left her alone in the world. But she was his wife; and, as the injury had been done to him, the punishment should follow from his hands! When he finds out who the sinner was, he does not proclaim him and hold him up to disgrace; he does not crush the almost adored minister of the gospel by declaring the sinner's trespass. He simply lives with his enemy in the same house, attacking not the man's body,—to which, indeed, he acts as a wise physician,—but his conscience, till we see the wretch writhing beneath the treatment.

Hester sees it too, and her strength, which suffices for the bearing of her own misery, fails her almost to fainting as she understands the condition of the man she has loved. Then there is a scene, the one graceful and pretty scene in the book, in which the two meet,—the two who were lovers,—and dare for a moment to think that they can escape. They come together in a wood, and she flings away, but for a moment, the badge of her shame, and lets down the long hair which has been hidden under her cap, and shines out before the reader for once,—just for that once,—as a lovely woman. She counsels him to fly, to go back across the waters to the old home whence he had come, and seek for rest away from the cruelty of his tyrant. When he pleads that he has no strength left to him for such action, then she declares that she will go with him and protect him and minister to him and watch over him with her strength. Yes; this woman proposes that she will then elope with the partner of her former sin. But no idea comes across the reader's mind of sinful love. The poor wretch can not live without service, and she will serve him. Were it herself that was concerned, she would remain there in her solitude, with the brand of her shame still open upon her bosom. But he can not go alone, and she too will therefore go.

As I have said before, the old man discovers the plot, and crushes their hopes simply by declaring that he will also be their companion. Whether there should have been this gleam of sunshine in the story the critic will doubt. . . . The extreme pain of the chronicle is mitigated for a moment. The reader almost fears that he is again about to enjoy the satisfaction of a happy ending. . . .

But through all this intensity of suffering, through this blackness of narrative, there is ever running a vein of drollery. As Hawthorne himself says, "a lively sense of the humorous again stole in among the solemn phantoms of her thought." He is always laughing at something with his weird, mocking spirit. The very children when they see Hester in the streets are supposed to speak of her in this wise: "Behold, verily, there is the woman of the scarlet letter. Come, therefore, and let us fling mud at her." Of some religious book he says, "It must have been a work of vast ability in the somniferous school of literature." "We must not always talk in the market-place of what happens to us in the forest," says even the sad mother to her child. Through it all there is a touch of burlesque,—not as to the suffering of the sufferers, but as to the great question whether it signifies much in what way we suffer, whether by crushing sorrows or little stings. Who would not sooner be Prometheus than a yesterday's tipsy man with this morning's sick-headache? In this way Hawthorne seems to ridicule the very woes which he expends himself in depicting.

As a novel "The House of the Seven Gables" is very inferior to "The Scarlet Letter." The cause of this inferiority would, I think, be plain to any one who had himself been concerned in the writing of novels. When Hawthorne proposed to himself to write "The Scarlet Letter," the plot of his story was clear to his mind. He wrote the book because he had the story strongly, lucidly manifest to his own imagination. In composing the other he was driven to search for a plot, and to make a story. "The Scarlet Letter" was written because he had it to write, and the other because he had to write it. The novelist will often find himself in the latter position. He has characters to draw, lessons to teach, philosophy perhaps which he wishes to expose, satire to express, humor to scatter abroad. These he can employ gracefully and easily if he have a story to tell. If he have none, he must concoct something of a story laboriously, when his lesson, his characters, his philosophy, his satire, and his humor will be less graceful and less easy. All the good things I have named are there in "The House of the Seven Gables"; but they are brought in with less artistic skill, because the author has labored over his plot, and never had it clear to his own mind.

The reader is not carried on by any intense interest in the story itself, and comes at last not much to care whether he does or does not understand the unraveling [of the mysteries]. He finds that his interest in the book lies

Perspectives

ROBERT E. SPILLER

HAWTHORNE'S EARLY LIFE was a long apprenticeship for a comparatively brief period of literary activity. He was thirty-three before the first of his collections of short stories appeared and forty-six before he wrote a successful novel. Yet he never once doubted that he must become an author. When his sea-captain father died in 1808, and the boy was shut in upon himself in the old house in Salem by his mother's devotion to a memory, he read Spenser and Milton and prepared with a tutor for Bowdoin College. His shyness was deeply rooted and was always present, whether he was living the life of a recluse or was joining quite naturally with his fellows. Biographers have had difficulty in reconciling his long period of withdrawal and apparent misanthropy with the accounts of his genial relations with his college friends Franklin Pierce, Henry Longfellow, and Horatio Bridge, and later with his wife and children. There is no inconsistency; the shy and introspective personality may very well be unusually gentle and outgoing when he is genuinely at ease. Hawthorne pitied rather than hated mankind; he was burdened rather than revolted by man's heritage of sin.

The twelve-year period of relative withdrawal from society, when he lived in Salem after his graduation from Bowdoin, was a period of deliberate preparation for his art. He read voluminously and wrote the experimental *Seven Tales of My Native Land,* all of which he presumably destroyed. His first published tale, *Fanshawe* (1828), might well have been destroyed also, except for its part self-portrait of the scholar-recluse grappling with the problem of living his own life and at the same time adjusting to society. In Fanshawe the worlds of thought and of reality were separate and irreconcilable; they were so for Hawthorne also, then and always. His personal story is one of a constant effort to adjust to living while preserving his own spiritual integrity; his tales are various treatments of this major theme. Like Poe, he made his best adjustment by the creation of art rather than, like Thoreau, by the arbitrary shaping of an independent course of life.

Success came when he learned how to get perspective on his problem by pushing it back into his own racial and national past. Living in the town where the witch trials had taken place, and involved in them through his direct ancestor Judge William Hathorne, he found it easy to become completely immersed in Salem history and in the lives of the Puritan colonists. Their problem was his problem, his problem theirs. The fact that with them sin was an awful reality while with him it was a psychological obsession only made them the perfect instruments to receive his skeptical speculations. His intro-spection could be exhibited in a fictional frame. He turned naturally to the extreme form of symbolism, the moral allegory, as the most nearly perfect medium available to his desperate needs for confession and for secrecy. Here he could say what he wanted to say and yet hide behind his symbols.

Gradually he was drawn out into the world by his old friend Horatio Bridge who arranged for the publication of the first volume of *Twice-Told Tales* in 1837 (second series, 1842) and by Sophia Peabody whom he married in 1842. Meanwhile he had sought a means of earning a living with the least possible concession to Mammon. An experimental residence at the Utopian colony of Brook Farm was wholly unsuccessful, probably because his motives were practical rather than Utopian. A post in the Boston Custom House was uncomfortable but adequate to his immediate needs. Only in the romantic interlude at the Old Manse in Concord, where he took his fragile bride, does he seem to have been completely happy. In 1846 he published his third volume of tales, *Mosses from an Old Manse,* and returned to the slavery of the Custom House once more, this time at Salem. He was not writing the kind of story that at any time—and much less at that time—would supply the means of livelihood. . . .

There was only one more collection of short tales, *The Snow-Image and Other Twice-Told Tales* (1852), not counting the collections in the "Tanglewood" series for boys and girls. The range of Hawthorne's art in this genre is not great, and he tends to repeat his characters, his themes, his scenes. The unity that Poe demanded, Hawthorne achieved in a dozen or more tales, but variety is lacking. It was his publisher-friend James T. Fields who came to his rescue in 1850 with the suggestion that he would gain more readers by a longer story. In *The Scarlet Letter* Hawthorne discovered not only a greater range, but an even greater depth. The characters of Hester Prynne and her lover, the Reverend Arthur Dimmesdale, are the first to step out from the frame of his speculations and become people in their own right. The theme is the now familiar one of a sin committed before the story opens and of the unfolding of the conse-quences of that act in the lives of a group of people. Here the sin is adultery, but Hawthorne does not share the absolute morality of the Puritan community which demands perpetual penance in the wearing of the scarlet letter "A." On the level of the higher and almost pagan morality which he seems instinctively to favor, Hester by her public and constant confession gains a kind of purity and strength which is not otherwise found in this God-fearing people. Dim-mesdale, on the other hand, in keeping his part in the sin a secret while he appears to the world as a spiritual leader, suffers a moral degeneration that leads to his breakdown and death. Strangely enough, the third member of the triangle, the wronged husband Roger Chillingworth, is made the real villain of the piece in that he commits Hawthorne's sin of sins, the violation of the human heart, by exerting his almost hypnotic control over the young minister and deliberately causing his ruin. The codified morality of the Puritan commu-nity becomes in this strange tale the social complex against which the natural morality of earthly love revolts. The tragedy lies in the failure of that protest, even though the principals, the two who have committed the social crime, are ennobled by their ordeal. As Christian tragedy, the pattern of the action is set by the theme of the Fall, but salvation comes through acknowledgment of Satan rather than of God. Hester is, of course, condemned to eternal torment by this dispensation; but the tale is also a Greek tragedy because she is the woman of earth who has defied man-made law and has risen to heroic stature through the tragic flaw that must at last destroy as well as ennoble her. Hawthorne wrote better than he knew, and better than he could write again.

The ambiguity of his own position was completely revealed in this short and perfect work of art. He had fully accepted the terms of his material and had allowed his characters to state their own cases, exercising only an aesthetic control over their actions. His moral disinterestedness was much more nearly perfect than he imagined. In spite of himself, he had become in ethics the total skeptic who could view calmly the paradox of human will working its own destruction. He had joined society and his inherited faith in condemning Hester at the same time that he revealed why not only he but all men must love her.

Never again was he so detached from the life of which he wrote, and never again was he master of so concentrated an artistry. In the Preface to his next novel, *The House of the Seven Gables* (1851), he makes explicit the method that up to now was instinctive. He is writing, he tells us, a Romance, in distinction to a Novel which must "aim at a very minute fidelity, not merely to the possible, but to the probable and ordinary course of man's experience." A Romance, as a work of art, must also subject itself rigidly to laws, and sins unpardonably in so far as it may swerve aside from the truth of the human heart, but within these limits it has fairly a right to present that truth under circumstances to a great extent of the author's own choosing or creation.

Hawthorne takes full advantage of his writer's freedom in the loving care with which he reconstructs the past of his native Salem and in his choice of a House rather than a person for his central character. The House is a family as well as a physical fact, as it was in Poe's tale of the House of Usher, and the theme is a curse which carries down through the generations. The wrong that the original Colonel Pyncheon did to the revengeful Matthew Maule is visited upon the nineteenth century Judge Pyncheon and his pathetic cousins Hepzibah and Clifford. In leaving the house, Holgrave, the descendant of Maule, finally absolves the now crumbling mansion of its curse, but its life is past. A more sustained piece of writing than the last, this novel—or Romance— does not quite reach the same depths of understanding because it relies more on setting and theme, less on characterization. It tends to become diffuse where *The Scarlet Letter* was concentrated, panoramic where the earlier work was focused with cruel concentration; but its tragic intensity is no less.

The next two novels play further variations on the theme of conscience. Hawthorne's Brook Farm associates serve as models in *The Blithedale Romance* (1852) for a group of people who feed upon one another's hearts as they attempt to construct a social Utopia, but the two strong characters Zenobia and Holl- ingsworth fail to gain either Hawthorne's or the reader's allegiance, and the tragic outcome of the plot is therefore unconvincing. The delicately spiritual

Priscilla and the scholar-recluse Coverdale are by now too much in control of the writer's own view of life, and the tendency to rely on melodramatic circumstances to carry the theme of hypnotic violation of personality weakens what might have been a unique masterpiece of psychological analysis. There is probably no novel of the era in which the role of the subconscious is so fully apprehended, so little understood.

Hawthorne's last completed novel, *The Marble Faun* (1860), is a product of his years of residence in Liverpool as American consul and of his travels in Italy. The scene is modern Rome, but the characters and theme are transferred from Puritan New England. The writer's hope to make his novel popular as a sort of guidebook was realized by the imbedding of long descriptive passages in the narrative with the result of a further extenuation. The theme of sin, retribution, and salvation, at least in this world, through confession, provides a frame for an elaborate plot in which fantasy and melodramatic incidents play their full parts. The faun-like ears of Donatello who loses his innocence but gains humanity by the knowledge of evil are unconvincing, and the plot of murder and confession is never realized on the symbolic level; yet there is a sustained delight in this novel as in all the others. However dark his imagination, Hawthorne's life in the world of make-believe was always intense, and he is able to convey that enjoyment to his reader. There is a witchery about his longer works which sustains even this last great story, in spite of a gradual relaxing of the controls which had made his first romance his greatest. It is the power of the artist who knows at firsthand the passions and problems of which he writes, but is able to present them without himself becoming entangled in their web. The agency of his perspective was allegory which, because it is used primarily for aesthetic rather than moral purposes, serves to supply a symbolic level of meaning to the imagined events. In spite of his deep concern for morality as the major force in human affairs, Hawthorne, like Poe, achieved in his best work an aesthetic detachment that made it possible for him to give to American life, at the moment of its first cultural renaissance, a critical presentation in literary art.

From *The Cycle of American Literature: An Essay in Historical Criticism* (New York: Macmillan, 1955), pp. 79-81, 83-88.

HENRY JAMES, JR.

WHATEVER MAY have been Hawthorne's private lot, he has the importance of being the most beautiful and most eminent representative of a literature. The importance of the literature may be questioned, but at any rate, in the field of letters, Hawthorne is the most valuable example of the American genius. That genius has not, as a whole, been literary; but Hawthorne was on his limited scale a master of expression. He is the writer to whom his countrymen most confidently point when they wish to make a claim to have enriched the mother-tongue, and, judging from present appearances, he will long occupy this honourable position. . . . He was so modest and delicate a genius that we may fancy him appealing from the lonely honour of a representative attitude— perceiving a painful incongruity between his imponderable literary baggage and the large conditions of American life. Hawthorne, on the one side, is so subtle and slender and unpretending, and the American world, on the other, is so vast and various and substantial, that it might seem to the author of *The Scarlet Letter* and the *Mosses from an Old Manse,* that we render him a poor service in contrasting his proportions with those of a great civilization. But our author must accept the awkward as well as the graceful side of his fame; for he has the advantage of pointing a valuable moral. This moral is that the flower of art blooms only where the soil is deep, that it takes a great deal of history to produce a little literature, that it needs a complex social machinery to set a writer in motion. American civilization has hitherto had other things to do than to produce flowers, and before giving birth to writers it has wisely occupied itself with providing something for them to write about. Three or four beauti- ful plants of trans-Atlantic growth are the sum of what the world usually recognises, and in this modest nosegay the genius of Hawthorne is admitted to have the rarest and sweetest fragrance.

His very simplicity has been in his favour; it has helped him to appear complete and homogeneous. To talk of his being national would be to force the note and make a mistake of proportion; but he is, in spite of the absence of the realistic quality, intensely and vividly local. Out of the soil of New England he sprang—in a crevice of that immitigable granite he sprouted and bloomed. Half of the interest that he possesses for an American reader with any turn for analysis must reside in his latent New England savour; and I think it no more than just to say that whatever entertainment he may yield to those who know him at a distance, it is an almost indispensable condition of properly appreciating him to have received a personal impression of the manners, the morals, indeed of the very climate, of the great region of which the remarkable city of Boston is the metropolis. The cold, bright air of New England seems to blow through his pages, and these, in the opinion of many people, are the medium in which it is most agreeable to make the acquaintance of that tonic atmosphere. As to whether it is worth while to seek to know something of New England in order to extract a more intimate quality from *The House of Seven Gables* and *The Blithedale Romance*, I need not pronounce; but it is certain that a considerable observation of the society to which these productions were more directly addressed is a capital preparation for enjoying them. I have alluded to the absence in Hawthorne of that quality of realism which is now so much in fashion, an absence in regard to which there will of course be more to say; and yet I think I am not fanciful in saying that he testifies to the sentiments of the society in which he flourished almost as pertinently (proportions observed) as Balzac and some of his descendants—MM. Flaubert and Zola—testify to the manners and morals of the French people. He was not a man with a literary theory; he was guiltless of a system, and I am not sure that he had ever heard of Realism, this remarkable compound having (although it was invented some time earlier) come into general use only since his death. He had certainly not proposed to himself to give an account of the social idiosyncrasies of his fellow-citizens, for his touch on such points is always light and vague, he has none of the apparatus of an historian, and his shadowy style of portraiture never suggests a rigid standard of accuracy. Nevertheless, he virtually offers the most vivid reflection of New England life that has found its way into literature. His value in this respect is not diminished by the fact that he has not attempted to portray the usual Yankee of comedy, and that he has been almost culpably indifferent to his opportunities for commemorating the variations of colloquial English that may be observed in the New World. His characters do not express themselves in the dialect of the *Biglow Papers*—their language, indeed, is apt to be too elegant, too delicate. They are not portraits of actual types, and in their phraseology there is nothing imitative. But none the less, Hawthorne's work savours thoroughly of the local soil—it is redolent of the social system in which he had his being. . . .

This is the real charm of Hawthorne's writing—this purity and spontaneity and naturalness of fancy. For the rest, it is interesting to see how it borrowed a particular colour from the other faculties that lay near it—how the imagination, in this capital son of the old Puritans, reflected the hue of the more purely moral part, of the dusky, overshadowed conscience. The conscience, by no fault of its own, in every genuine offshoot of that sombre lineage, lay under the shadow of the sense of *sin*. This darkening cloud was no essential part of the nature of the individual; it stood fixed in the general moral heaven under which he grew up and looked at life. It projected from above, from outside, a black patch over his spirit, and it was for him to do what he could with the black patch. There were all sorts of possible ways of dealing with it; they depended upon the personal temperament. Some natures would let it lie as it fell, and contrive to be tolerably comfortable beneath it. Others would groan and sweat and suffer; but the dusky blight would remain, and their lives would be lives of misery. Here and there an individual, irritated beyond endurance, would throw it off in anger, plunging probably into what would be deemed deeper abysses of depravity. Hawthorne's way was the best; for he contrived, by an exquisite process, best known to himself, to transmute this heavy moral burden into the very substance of the imagination, to make it evaporate in the light and charming fumes of artistic production. But Hawthorne, of course, was exceptionally fortunate; he 'had his genius to help him. Nothing is more curious and interesting than this almost exclusively *imported* character of the sense of sin in Hawthorne's mind; it seems to exist there merely for an artistic or literary purpose. He had ample cognizance of the Puritan conscience; it was his natural heritage; it was reproduced in him; looking into his soul, he found it there. But his relation to it was only, as one may say, intellectual; it was not moral and theological. He played with it, and used it as a pigment; he treated it, as the metaphysicians say, objectively. He was not discomposed, disturbed, haunted by it, in the manner of its usual and regular victims, who had not the little postern door of fancy to slip through, to the other side of the wall. It was, indeed, to his imaginative vision, the great fact of man's nature; the light element that had been mingled with his own composition always clung to this rugged prominence of moral responsibility, like the mist that hovers about the mountain. It was a necessary condition for a man of Hawthorne's stock that if his imagination should take license to amuse itself, it should at least select this grim precinct of the Puritan morality for its play-ground. He speaks of the dark disapproval with which his old ancestors, in the case of their coming to life, would see him trifling himself away as a story-teller. But how far more darkly would they have frowned could they have understood that he had converted the very principle of their own being into one of his toys!

It will be seen that I am far from being struck with the justice of that view of the author of the *Twice-Told Tales,* which is so happily expressed by the French critic to whom I alluded at an earlier stage of this essay. To speak of Hawthorne, as M. Emile Montégut does, as a *romancier pessimiste,* seems to me very much beside the mark. He is no more a pessimist than an optimist, though he is certainly not much of either. He does not pretend to conclude, or to have a philosophy of human nature; indeed, I should even say that at bottom he does not take human nature as hard as he may seem to do. "His bitterness," says M. Montégut, "is without abatement, and his bad opinion of man is without compensation. . . . His little tales have the air of confessions which the soul makes to itself; they are so many little slaps which the author applies to our face." This, it seems to me, is to exaggerate almost immeasurably the reach of Hawthorne's relish of gloomy subjects. What pleased him in such subjects was their picturesqueness, their rich duskiness of colour, their chiaroscuro; but they were not the expression of a hopeless, or even of a predominantly melancholy, feeling about the human soul. Such at least is my own impression. He is to a considerable degree ironical—this is part of his charm—part even, one may say, of his brightness; but he is neither bitter nor cynical—he is rarely even what I should call tragical. There have certainly been story-tellers of a gayer and lighter spirit; there have been observers more humorous, more hilarious—though on the whole Hawthorne's observation has a smile in it oftener than may at first appear; but there has rarely been an observer more serene, less agitated by what he sees and less disposed to call things deeply into question. As I have already intimated, his Note-Books are full of this simple and almost childlike serenity. That dusky pre-occupation with the misery of human life and the wickedness of the human heart which such a critic as M. Emile Montégut talks about, is totally absent from them; and if we may suppose a person to have read these Diaries before looking into the tales, we may be sure that such a reader would be greatly surprised to hear the author described as a disappointed, disdainful genius. "This marked love of cases of conscience," says M. Montégut; "this taciturn, scornful cast of mind; this habit of seeing sin everywhere, and hell always gaping open; this dusky gaze bent always upon a damned world, and a nature draped in mourning; these lonely conversations of the imagination with the conscience; this pitiless analysis resulting from a perpetual examination of one's self, and from the tortures of a heart closed before men and open to God—all these elements of the Puritan character have passed into Mr. Hawthorne, or, to speak more justly, have *filtered* into him, through a long succession of generations." This is a very pretty and very vivid account of Hawthorne, superficially considered; and it is just such a view of the case as would commend itself most easily and most naturally to a hasty critic. It is all true indeed, with a difference; Hawthorne was all that M. Montégut says, *minus* the conviction. The old Puritan moral sense, the consciousness of sin and hell, of the fearful nature of our responsibilities and the savage character of our Taskmaster—these things had been lodged in the mind of a man of Fancy, whose fancy had straightway begun to take liberties and play tricks with them—to judge them (Heaven forgive him!) from the poetic and aesthetic point of view, the point of view of entertainment and irony. This absence of conviction makes the difference; but the difference is great.

From *Hawthorne* (New York: Harper & Brothers, 1879), pp. 2-5, 56-60.

LEWIS E. GATES

IT USED to be the fashion a generation ago to have much to say about the morbidness of the life that Hawthorne's stories portray. But of late years the decadents have been in their romances so ingeniously busy with disease and death that to turn back to Hawthorne seems like returning to nature—to what is normal and healthy and sanative. It may, indeed, be true that Hawthorne had a hypertrophied conscience, and that the portrayal of life seemed to him chiefly worth while because it gave him a chance to indulge that conscience in its somewhat morbid desire to be troublesome. But, after all, to have an overanxious conscience is a more human state of affairs than to have, as is so often true of the decadents, no conscience at all, or to have one only to the end that clever defiance of it may lead to finely calculated discords in the music of art. Just here lies the difference between the novels of Hawthorne and the stories that modern decadence is so liberal with. In both forms of art, sin, disease, death, the grisliest facts of human destiny are perpetually in evidence; but Hawthorne is sincere in dealing with them, and measures their results and computes their meaning in terms of normal life and the conventional moral consciousness, whereas modern decadents are primarily concerned to juggle out of the evil facts of life and their impact on our moral nature some new fantastic artistic effect, and care not a doit for the ethical point of view.

It is amusing to find Hawthorne now and then having an inkling of the existence of the primrose path of decadence, or coquetting with the notion of irresponsibility. In the *Blithedale Romance* he seems nearest to defying his conscience and being recklessly studious of artistic effects for their own dear sakes. Miles Coverdale, who tells the story, is, as he assures us, "a devoted epicure of his own emotions." In one place, after describing a mood in which "the actual world" was robbed for him "of its solidity," Coverdale tells us, in a self-satisfied way, that he "resolved to pause and enjoy the moral sillabub" of the mood "until it was quite dissolved away." In another place he confesses to the habit of observing and analyzing from a distance the characters of his fellows, and he is evidently somewhat proud of his speculative and half-cynical detachment. "It is not, I apprehend, a healthy kind of mental occupation," he declares, with apparently a pleasant sense of abnormality, "to devote one's self too exclusively to the study of individual men and women." Yet despite a few such superficial symptoms of dilettantism, Coverdale has a very respectable conscience, which insinuates its vigorous prejudices into his interpretation of the lives and actions he is observing and reporting.

What is true of Coverdale is true in a yet higher degree of Hawthorne's other characters; sooner or later they all become acutely aware of having fostered or violated a Puritan conscience—with the possible exception of Zenobia; and on her, poor woman! Hawthorne, while he portrays her, keeps fixed a kind of evil eye, which ultimately drives her into suicide as the only fitting expiation for her venturesome originality. As for Donatello, in the *Marble Faun,* who is at the start ostensibly the very type of unmoral humanity, he is, despite all his flourish of animality, never anything else than a thoroughly well-tamed creature, fit to caper in a lady's chamber. His wildness is a hothouse wildness, a studio wildness, a manipulated, carefully fostered wildness, that is useful only for purposes of ornament and demonstration. When one really contemplates Donatello in the light of modern science, there is something curiously grotesque in trying to regard Hawthorne's Faun as the Missing Link or as Primeval Man before he evolved a conscience. There is more of outdoors in one verse of Walt Whitman's than in all Hawthorne's pages about Donatello.

No; the simple truth is that Hawthorne is in all his romances normal in spite of himself, and persistently moral and ethical in his interests despite his constitutional unsociability, his contempt for conventions, and his overweening imaginativeness. He is ruled by his Puritan ancestors, and in his most fantastic individual dreams is loyal to inherited moral prejudices. His earnestness of purpose and his unfailing moral scrupulousness give to his dream-world and its shadowy populace a genuineness and cogency which the art of the decadents, dealing as it does in many of the same *motifs,* never rivals.

Still, it remains true that not more with Hawthorne than with the decadents are we in the actual world of every day. Hawthorne is a dreamer who "dreams *true,*" but who, nevertheless, merely *dreams,* and whose world has the delicate intangibility of all dream-worlds. We never escape, in reading Hawthorne's romances, from the temperament of the author, and from his unobtrusive but persistent imaginative control. He creates for a purpose, and in each romance he subdues to this purpose the background, the incident, the plot, the characters, and even the imagery and phrasing. The thoroughness with which his generating purpose runs through every detail and word of a romance, and fashions and tempers and unifies all to a single predetermined end, is one of the most convincing proofs of Hawthorne's power as an imaginative artist. There is no piecemeal working in Hawthorne—none of the haphazard procedure that takes details and suggestions good-naturedly as chance offers them and weaves them dextrously, as Thackeray, for example, is wont to do, into a motley web of fiction. Each of Hawthorne's long romances is a perfectly wrought work of art, wherein every part is nicely aware of all the rest and of the central purpose and total effect.

Hawthorne is a master spinner of beautiful webs, and the most rabid devotee of art for art's sake cannot well refuse to enjoy the fineness and consistency of his designs, the continuity and firmness of his texture, and the richness and depth of his tinting. The pattern, to be sure, always contains a moral for apt pupils. But though Hawthorne dreams in terms of the ten commandments, he dreams beauty none the less; and, indeed, for some of us who still believe that life is greater than art, his dreams are all the more fascinating artistically because they are deeply, darkly, beautifully true. . . .

In all his romances Hawthorne is more or less plainly in pursuit of some moral or spiritual truth. In the desire to illustrate such a truth is to be found the originating motive of each of his longer works. The *Scarlet Letter* is the Romance of Expiation, done in deeply glowing colours against the dark, sullen background of the Puritan temperament. *The House of the Seven Gables* is the Romance of Heredity. The colours are gray and sombre, with some pretty fantastic detail in pale rose and green where Phoebe's tender girlishness or womanliness appears. The *Marble Faun* is the Romance of the Mystery of Evil: It is the most elaborate of all Hawthorne's stories, and as a work of art is nearer lacking unity of tone and design, because of the archaeological and landscape detail of which the author is so lavish. Yet even here the background, though elaborate, has propriety. The story deals in symbolic form with the deepest mystery of human destiny—the origin and the meaning of evil; and the background for the action is Rome, the very stones of whose streets tell tales of the struggles toward good and toward evil of many races of men. Rome, with its long perspectives through a picturesque past, is the symbol of civilized man in all his history, from the far away origin of society down to latter-day love of anarchy. Against this background is depicted the symbolic fate of Donatello and Hilda and Miriam, as types of the human will in its relation to evil.

For the analyst of novelists' methods there is a real delight to be won from noting how consistent Hawthorne is in constructing his stories. He works invariably just as he ought to work to suit the theorist's notions. Being a creator of allegorical romances, he ought to work from within his own mind out toward the world of actual fact, for which world he should have a fine disdain. His main purpose should be the creation and illustration of moral effects. In an essay on Hawthorne's Tales, Poe has very happily laid down the law for this kind of fiction. . . . All these prescriptions, which, according to Poe, should govern the short tale, will be found duly observed in Hawthorne's long romances. In tale and romance Hawthorne's methods are nearly the same. His imagination, in its dreamy play over the records of the remote drama of life, has been fascinated by some one of its typical and oft-recurring aspects—the bitterness of the expiation of sin, the tragic oppression wherewith the vices and even the virtues of the past weigh down on the innocent present. Such a large aspect of life usually carries with it into the dark-chamber of Hawthorne's mind some typical man or woman whose character and fate incarnate for him, with picturesque detail, the special truths about life that for the time being preoccupy him. From these original elements, the action of the story and all subordinate detail gradually shape themselves forth and take shadowy form, never with the wish or the hope of bringing the reader close to some glaring piece of actual life, but always with the aim of enveloping him subduingly in an atmosphere of spiritual emotion, and of offering him unobtrusively at every moment, in the acts, in the thoughts and feelings of the actors, in the byways and vistas of nature, in the very air that he breathes, hints and symbols of certain large truths about human life and human endeavour. The regions where the action takes place are oftenest nameless; they are in dreamland—"vaporous, unaccountable, forlorn of light;" they are not verifiable as actual corners of the world-ball, unless they are already so instinct with romance as to be fit to conspire with the author's purpose and help on the moral necromancy. The people that inhabit this dream-world are "goblins of flesh and blood"; they are spirited up before us out of an unknown past. Priscilla, Hawthorne assures us, seemed to have "fallen out of the clouds"; Miriam's past and even large parts of her present are tantalizingly unverifiable. The gossip of those who surround the principal actors tends to veil them still more deftly in a dim cloud of strangeness, rather than to expound their personalities with scientific accuracy, as would happen in a modern realistic story. We never know thoroughly the details of the lives of Chillingworth or Donatello; we are kept in uncertainty about them through surmises and suspicions that run in the story from lip to lip. What is sure about such characters is their pursuit of a few symbolic purposes which serve to fit them unerringly into the large design of the fable. Donatello is all the time busied with the process of getting a soul. Judge Pyncheon is bent on selfish triumph at all costs, in pursuit of hereditary schemes of aggrandizement. Dimmesdale writhes his way pallidly through the *Scarlet Letter,*—hand on heart,—the visible symbol of repentance. Neither in these characters nor in any others is there an attempt at thoroughness or minuteness of realization, or at any delicate complication of motives or at scientific analysis. Hawthorne keeps his characterization carefully free from the intricacies of actual life, and preserves uncontaminate the large outlines and glowing colours of his simplified men and women. Even in speech the people of his stories are nicely unreal; his workmen are choice in their English, and his children lisp out sentences that are prettily modelled. Here, as so often, Hawthorne cares nothing for crude fact.

His world, too, is a world where symbols are as frequent as in the happy days before Newton, the arch-foe of symbols, unwove the rainbow. The main action itself of each romance is one great symbol, and it germinates persistently in minor symbols. Scarlet letters flash out unexpectedly, even on the face of the heavens; the House of the Seven Gables visibly shadows Hepzibah, Clifford, and Phoebe with the evil influences of the past; Hilda's doves encircle her and her tower with suggestions of unsullied innocence. So, too, Hawthorne's characters themselves have features or tricks of manner that mark them out as symbolic and as meaning more than meets the eye; Donatello's ears, Priscilla's tremulous, listening look, Dimmesdale's persistent clutching at his heart, tease the reader into a continuous sense of the haunted duplicity of the world in which Hawthorne keeps him. In each of Hawthorne's romances the world and its inhabitants echo and re-echo a single importunate thought.

Of course, all this is very sadly removed from the kind of art that the realists of recent years have instructed us to delight in. No one of literary experience can cheat himself into fancying as he reads Hawthorne that he is having to do with real men or women or treading the solid ground of fact. He is continually aware that the world he moves in has been tampered with. Nevertheless, Hawthorne's fiction is bound to remain for most readers—both for uncritical readers and for readers of cultivation and discernment, even for those of them who are completely familiar with the best work of the modern realists—a permanent source of delight. And this is true for various reasons. The lover of skilful technique, whatever his theory of the ultimate aims of fiction, must relish the beauty of Hawthorne's workmanship. No one can gainsay Hawthorne's skill of execution, the largeness and symmetry of his designs, his delicately sure manipulation of detail, the intelligence of his methods when his ends are once granted, the freedom and uninterruptedness of his draughting, and the perfect graduation of his tones. Then, too, his romances have an abiding source of charm, whatever the fluctuations of fashion, in the fineness and nobleness of the temperament in terms of which they make life over. Doubtless this temperament has its limitations. Hawthorne's conscience was a familiar spirit that would not be laid, and Hawthorne allowed himself to be driven to the almost invariable study of pathological states of soul and the analysis of guilt and expiation, until a reader is tempted to exclaim that life for Hawthorne is seven-eighths conduct and the other eighth remorse. Still, through all this inherited Puritanic gloom there runs continually an unsubduable love for human nature, which makes the world of Hawthorne's stories a hospitable region, and gives the reader a sense of well-being even in the midst of the misdeeds and repentances through which he makes his way. He feels that he breathes a genuine atmosphere of human sympathy; tenderness and love, all the elemental affections that form the abidingly worthy substance of human nature, are generously active in Hawthorne's men and women—his people are real enough for that; and, moreover, Hawthorne, the author, bears himself toward all the folk of his mimic drama with large-hearted charity and indefatigable faith in the essential rightness of the universe. The romances are, to quote Hawthorne's own words, "true to the human heart," and the human heart, as Hawthorne interprets it, is a very lovable and love-disseminating organ. For their rich, strong humanity, Hawthorne's romances will long be gratefully read by all who either naively or instructedly believe life to be worth living. . . .

What oftenest disturbs the modern and exacting reader of Hawthorne, and rouses him unpleasantly from his dream, is Hawthorne's abuse of symbols. Now and then, Hawthorne's instinct fails him in making the nice distinction between art and artifice. In his creation of atmosphere and search for effect he is occasionally obvious and cheap, and seems to tamper needlessly with facts and with the laws of nature. The heat of the scarlet letter becomes after a time oppressive; the display of the A in the heavens, during the scene on the scaffold, seems merely a theatrical bid for a shiver. The shadow that is asserted always to have rested on Chillingworth, even in the sunshine, seems the result of a gratuitous juggling with the laws of light. Now and again, in such cases as these, Hawthorne makes us aware that he is playing tricks on our souls. Matthew Arnold has quoted Sainte-Beuve as somewhere saying that every kind of art has its characteristic defect, and that the defect of Romantic art is *le faux.*

From this falseness Hawthorne keeps, on the whole, wonderfully free; and yet at times he is betrayed into it. . . .

Finally, it must be admitted that Hawthorne has never studied or portrayed sympathetically a man or woman of real intellectual quality; he has never put before us a first-rate mind in perfect working order, nor anywhere traced out, subtly and convincingly, the refinements of the intellectual life. It is not simply that he has never given us a genuine man of the world; of course, his method and temperament alike forbade that. From the very nature of Hawthorne's art, a man of the world, had Hawthorne tried to portray him, would have become a man out of the world. But why should not Hawthorne have portrayed, at least once in a way, a thoroughly intellectual man or woman? a man or woman whose mind was well disciplined, brilliant, and controlling? Nowhere has he done this. His men, the moment they grow accomplished, drift into morbidness or villainy—hunt the philosopher's stone, become grotesque philanthropists, take to mesmerism or alchemy or unwise experiments in matrimony. Hawthorne's fiction seems really somewhat vitiated by Romantic distrust of scholarship, of mental acuteness, and of whatever savours of the pride of intellect. This bias in his nature must be borne in mind when one is considering the shallowness and defectiveness of the individual characterization in his novels—a shallowness and defectiveness which, as has been noted, are involved in his essentially romantic conception of the art of fiction.

Yet, when all these disturbing elements in our enjoyment of Hawthorne have been allowed for, there remains a vast fund of often almost unalloyed delight to be won from his writings. Moreover, this delight seems likely to increase rather than grow less. At present, Hawthorne is at a decided disadvantage, because, while remote enough to seem in trifles here and there archaic, he is yet not remote enough to escape contemporary standards or to be read with imaginative historical allowances and sympathy, as Richardson or Defoe is read. Hawthorne's romances have the human quality and the artistic beauty that ensure survival; and in a generation or two, when the limitations of the Romantic ideal and the scope of Romantic methods have become historically clear in all men's minds, Hawthorne's novels will be read with an even surer sense than exists to-day of that beauty of form and style and that tender humanity which come from the individuality of their author, and with a more tolerant comprehension of the imperfectness of equipment and occasional faults of manner that were the result of his environment and age.

From "Hawthorne" in *Studies and Appreciations* (New York: Macmillan, 1900), pp. 92-109.

PAUL ELMER MORE

RARELY HAS a writer shown greater skill in self-criticism than Hawthorne, except where modesty caused him to lower the truth, and in ascribing this lack of passion to his works [*Twice-Told Tales*] he has struck what will seem to many the keynote of their character. When he says, however, that they are wanting in depth, he certainly errs through modesty. Many authors, great and small, display a lack of passion, but perhaps no other in all the hierarchy of poets who deal with moral problems has treated these problems, on one side at least, so profoundly as our New England romancer; and it is just this peculiarity of Hawthorne, so apparently paradoxical, which gives him his unique place among writers.

Consider for a moment *The Scarlet Letter*:the pathos of the subject, and the tragic scenes portrayed. All the world agrees that here is a masterpiece of mortal error and remorse; we are lost in admiration of the author's insight into the suffering human heart; yet has any one ever shed a tear over that inimitable romance? I think not. The book does not move us to tears; it awakens no sense of shuddering awe such as follows the perusal of the great tragedies of literature; it is not emotional, in the ordinary acceptance of the word, yet shallow or cold it certainly is not. . . .

What curious trait in his writing, what strange attitude of the man toward the moral struggles and agony of human nature, is this that sets him apart from other novelists? I purpose to show how this is due to one dominant motive running through all his tales,—a thought to a certain extent peculiar to himself, and so persistent in its repetition that, to one who reads Hawthorne carefully, his works seem to fall together like the movements of a great symphony built upon one imposing theme. . . .

Other poets of the past have excelled him in giving expression to certain problems of our inner life, and in stirring the depths of our emotional nature; but not in the tragedies of Greece, or the epics of Italy, or the drama of Shakespeare will you find any presentation of this one truth of the penalty of solitude laid upon the human soul so fully and profoundly worked out as in the romances of Hawthorne. It would be tedious to take up each of his novels and tales and show how this theme runs like a sombre thread through them all, yet it may be worth while to touch on a few prominent examples.

Shortly after leaving college, Hawthorne published a novel which his maturer taste, with propriety, condemned. Despite the felicity of style which seems to have come to Hawthorne by natural right, *Fanshawe* is but a crude and conventional story. Yet the book is interesting if only to show how at the very outset the author struck the keynote of his life's work. The hero of the tale is the conventional student that figures in romance, wasted by study, and isolated from mankind by his intellectual ideals. "He had seemed, to others and to himself, a solitary being, upon whom the hopes and fears of ordinary men were ineffectual." The whole conception of the story is a commonplace, yet a commonplace relieved by a peculiar quality in the language which even in this early attempt predicts the stronger treatment of his chosen theme when the artist shall have mastered his craft. There is, too, something memorable in the parting scene between the hero and heroine, where Fanshawe, having earned Ellen's love, deliberately surrenders her to one more closely associated with the world, and himself goes back to his studies and his death.

From this youthful essay let us turn at once to his latest work. . . . In the fragment of *The Dolliver Romance* we have, wrought out with all the charm of Hawthorne's maturest style, a picture of isolation caused, not by the exclusive ambitions of youth, but by old age and the frailty of human nature. No extract or comment can convey the effect of these chapters of minute analysis, with their portrait of the old apothecary dwelling in the time-eaten mansion, whose windows look down on the graves of children and grandchildren he had outlived and laid to rest. With his usual sense of artistic contrast, Hawthorne sets a picture of golden-haired youth by the side of withered eld. . . .

Again, in describing the loneliness that separates old age from the busy current of life, Hawthorne has recourse to a picture which he employed a number of times, and which seems to have been drawn from his own experience and to have haunted his dreams. It is the picture of a bewildered man walking the populous streets, and feeling utterly lost and estranged in the crowd. So the old doctor "felt a dreary impulse to elude the people's observation, as if with a sense that he had gone irrevocably out of fashion; . . . or else it was that nightmare feeling which we sometimes have in dreams, when we seem to find ourselves wandering through a crowded avenue, with the noonday sun upon us, in some wild extravagance of dress or nudity." We are reminded by the words of Hawthorne's own habit, during his early Salem years, of choosing to walk abroad at night when no one could observe him, and of his trick in later life of hiding in the Concord woods rather than face a passer-by on the road.

Between *Fanshawe,* with its story of the seclusion caused by youthful ambition, and *The Dolliver Romance,* with its picture of isolated old age, there may be found in the author's successive works every form of solitude incident to human existence. I believe no single tale, however short or insignificant, can be named in which, under one guise or another, this recurrent idea does not appear. It is as if the poet's heart were burdened with an emotion that unconsciously dominated every faculty of his mind; he walked through life like a man possessed. . . . Truly a curse is upon us; our life is rounded with impassable emptiness; the stress of youth, the feebleness of age, all the passions and desires of manhood, lead but to this inevitable solitude and isolation of spirit. . . .

It is, indeed, characteristic of this solitude of spirit that it presents itself now as the original sin awakening Heaven's wrath, and again as itself the penalty imposed upon the guilty soul: which is but Hawthorne's way of portraying evil and its retribution as simultaneous,—nay, as one and the same thing.

[*The Scarlet Letter*] is a story of intertangled love and hatred working out in four human beings the same primal curse,—love and hatred so woven together that in the end the author asks whether the two passions be not, after all, the same, since each renders one individual dependent upon another for his spiritual food, and each is in a way an attempt to break through the boundary that separates soul from soul. From the opening scene at the prison door, which, "like all that pertains to crime, seemed never to have known a youthful era," to the final scene on the scaffold, where the tragic imagination of the author speaks with a power barely surpassed in the books of the world, the whole plot of the romance moves about this one conception of our human isolation as the penalty of transgression. . . .

Morbid in any proper sense of the word Hawthorne cannot be called, except in so far as throughout his life he cherished one dominant idea, and that a peculiar state of mental isolation which destroys the illusions leading to action, and so tends at last to weaken the will; and there are, it must be confessed, signs in the maturer age of Hawthorne that his will actually succumbed to the attacks of this subtle disillusionment. But beyond this there is in his work no taint of unwholesomeness, unless it be in itself unwholesome to be possessed by one absorbing thought. We have no reason to discredit his own statement: "When I write anything that I know or suspect is morbid, I feel as though I had told a lie." Nor was he even a mystery-monger: the mysterious element in his stories, which affects some prosaic minds as a taint of morbidness, is due to the intense symbolism of his thought, to the intrinsic and unconscious mingling of the real and the ideal. Like one of his own characters, he could "never separate the idea from the symbol in which it manifests itself." Yet the idea is always there. He is strong both in analysis and generalisation; there is no weakening of the intellectual faculties. Furthermore, his pages are pervaded with a subtle ironical humour hardly compatible with morbidness,—not a boisterous humour that awakens laughter, but the mood, half quizzical and half pensive, of a man who stands apart and smiles at the foibles and pretensions of the world. Now and then there is something rare and unexpected in his wit, as, for example, in his comment on the Italian mosquitoes: "They are bigger than American mosquitoes; and if you crush them, after one of their feasts, it makes a terrific blood spot. It is a sort of suicide to kill them." And if there is to be found in his tales a fair share of disagreeable themes, yet he never confounds things of good and evil report, nor things fair and foul; the moral sense is intact. Above all, there is no undue appeal to the sensations or emotions.

Rather it is true, as we remarked in the beginning, that the lack of outward emotion, together with their poignancy of silent appeal, is a distinguishing mark of Hawthorne's writings. The thought underlying all his work is one to trouble the depths of our nature, and to stir in us the sombrest chords of brooding, but it does not move us to tears or passionate emotion: those affections are dependent on our social faculties, and are starved in the rarefied air of his genius. . . .

It needs but a slight acquaintance with his own letters and *Note-Books*, and with the anecdotes current about him, to be assured that never lived a man to whom ordinary contact with his fellows was more impossible, and that the mysterious solitude in which his fictitious characters move is a mere shadow of his own imperial loneliness of soul. . . .

He was not sceptical [of religion], to judge from his occasional utterances, but simply indifferent; the matter did not interest him. He was by right of inheritance a Puritan; all the intensity of the Puritan nature remained in him, and all the overwhelming sense of the heinousness of human depravity, but these, cut off from the old faith, took on a new form of their own. Where the Puritan teachers had fulminated the vengeance of an outraged God, Hawthorne saw only the infinite isolation of the errant soul. . . .

From "The Solitude of Nathaniel Hawthorne" in *Shelburne Essays, First Series* (New York: G. P. Putnam's Sons, 1904), pp. 22-50.

W. C. BROWNELL

ENERGY . . . is precisely the element most conspicuously lacking in the normal working of this [Hawthorne's] imagination which to Lowell recalls Shakespeare's. Repeatedly he seems to be on the point of exhibiting it, of moving us, that is to say; but, except, I think, in "The Scarlet Letter," he never quite does so. His unconquerable reserve steps in and turns him aside. He never crosses the line, never makes the attempt. He is too fastidious to attempt vigor and fail. His intellectual sensitiveness, to which failure in such an endeavor would be acutely palpable, prevents the essay. In the instance of "The Scarlet Letter," where he does achieve it, he does so as it were in spite of himself, and it is curious that he instinctively reestablishes his normal equilibrium by failing to appreciate his achievement. At least he prefers to it his "House of the Seven Gables." He is much more at home in amusing himself than in creating something. "I have sometimes," he says, "produced a singular and not unpleasing effect, so far as my own mind was concerned, by imagining a train of incidents in which the spirit and mechanism of the fairy legend should be combined with the characters and manners of familiar life." He was content if his effect was pleasing so far as his own mind was concerned. And his own mind was easily pleased with the kind of process he describes. That is, he follows his temperamental bent with tranquil docility instead of compelling it to serve him in the construction of some fabric of importance. The latter business demands energy and effort. And if he made so little effort it is undoubtedly because he had so little energy.

His genius was a reflective one. He loved to muse. Revery was a state of mind which he both indulged and applauded, and there can hardly be a more barren one for the production of anything more significant than conceits and fancies. Reality repelled him. What attracted him was mirage. Mirage is his specific aim, the explicit goal of his art—which thus becomes inevitably rather artistry than art. His practice is sustained by his theory. Speaking of a scene mirrored in a river he exclaims: "Which, after all, was the most real—the picture or the original?—the objects palpable to our grosser senses, or their apotheosis in the stream beneath? Surely the disembodied images stand in closer relation to the soul." If this were a figure expressive of the mirroring of nature by art it would be a happy one, though not convincing to those who believe that the artistic synthesis of nature should be more rather than less definite than its material. But it is not a figure. It is a statement of Hawthorne's preference for the vague and the undefined in nature itself as nearer to the soul.

Nearer to the soul of the poet it may be, not to that of the artist. The most idealizing artist can count on enough vagueness of his own—whether it handicap his effort or illumine his result in dealing with his material. And it is not near to the soul of the poet endowed with the architectonic faculty—the poet in the Greek sense, the maker. It is the congenial content of contemplation indeterminate and undirected.

The contemplative mind, the contemplative mood, are above all hospitable to fancy, and in fancy Hawthorne's mind and mood were wonderfully rich. He had but to follow its beckoning and entrust himself to its guidance to make a pretty satisfactory journey, at least so far as his own mind was concerned. The result was amazingly productive. How many "Mosses" and "Twice-Told Tales" are there? Certainly a prodigious number when one considers the narrowness of their range and their extraordinary variety within it. Their quality is singularly even, I think. Some of them—a few—are better than others, but mainly in more successfully illustrating their common quality. What this is Hawthorne himself sufficiently indicates in saying, "Instead of passion there is sentiment; and even in what purport to be pictures of actual life we have allegory." But his consciousness of his limitations does not exorcise them, though his candor, which is charming, wins our appreciation for their corresponding excellences.

Or, rather, no. It is so absolute as to make us feel a little ungracious at our inability to take quite his view after all. After all, it is plain that he has a paternal feeling for them that it is a little difficult to share. Sentiment replaces passion, it is true. But the sentiment is pale for sentiment. It is sentiment insufficiently *senti*. Allegory, it is true, replaces reality, but the allegory itself is insufficiently real. The tales are not merely in a less effective, less robust, less substantial category than that which includes passion and actual life, but within their own category they are—most of them—unaccented and inconclusive. They are too faint in color and too frail in construction quite to merit the inference of Hawthorne's pretty deprecation. They have not "the pale tint of flowers that blossomed in too retired a shade." They are hardly flowers at all, but grasses and ferns. And while he exaggerates in saying that "if opened in the sunshine" they are "apt to look exceedingly like a volume of blank pages," he is distinctly optimistic in thinking that they would gain greatly by being read "in the clear, brown, twilight atmosphere" in which they were written, and that they cannot always "be taken into the reader's mind without a shiver." They can—always. There is not a shiver in them. Their tone is lukewarm and their temper Laodicean. Witchery is precisely the quality they suggest but do not possess. Their atmosphere is not that of the clear brown twilight in which familiar objects are poetized, but that of the gray day in which they acquire monotone. The twilight and moonlight, so often figuratively ascribed to Hawthorne's genius, are in fact a superstition. There is nothing eerie or elfin about his genius. He is too much the master of it and directs it with a too voluntary control. Fertile as it is, its multifarious conceits and caprices are harnessed and handled with the light, firm hand of perfect precision and guided along a level course of extremely unbroken country. There is no greater sanity to be met with in literature than Hawthorne's. The wholesome constitution of his mind is inveterate and presides with unintermittent constancy in his prose. Now caprice, conducted by reason, infallibly incurs the peril of insipidity, and it is not to be denied that many of the tales settle comfortably into the category of the prosaic.

Why, then, have they their reputation, and why does one feel a little awkward and unsympathetic in confessing that he finds them dull? In the first place, the fondness of the public for them has been, in strict history, an acquired taste. They met with very little favor at first. The genial Longfellow praised them to deaf ears. After the appearance of "The Scarlet Letter" readers turned back to them in appreciative disposition and, as is usually the case under such circumstances, found or fancied in them what they looked for. But mainly they won and have kept their classic position, it is not to be doubted, because of their originality, their refinement, and their elevation. There is certainly nothing else like them; their taste is perfect; and, in general, they deal with some phase of the soul, some aspect or quality or transaction of the spiritual life. They are the echoes of no literary precedent, but as much Hawthorne's own as his physiognomy. They exhibit a literary fastidiousness not so much free from as absolutely dead to the manifold seductions of the meretricious, a literary breeding so admirable as to seem unconscious of the existence of vulgar expedients. And their informing purpose lies quite outside the material world and its sublunary phenomena. No small portion of their originality consists, indeed, in the association of their refinement and elevation with what we can now see is their mediocrity. Elsewhere in the world of fiction mediocrity is associated with anything but fineness of fibre and spirituality. The novelty of the combination in Hawthorne's case was disconcerting, and it is small wonder that for a time at least—for a generation, no doubt, so gradual is the readjustment of popular esteem of the unpopular—the importance of the "Twice-Told Tales" and the "Mosses" was argued from their distinction. Finally, some of them—too few, assuredly—are good stories.

Allegory is art only when its representation is as imaginatively real as its meaning. The mass of allegory—allegory strictly devoted to exposition and dependent upon exegesis, allegory explicitly so-called—is only incidentally art at all.

Hawthorne's is of this order. His subject is always something other than its substance. Everything means something else. Dealing with the outer world solely for the sake of the inner, he is careless of its character and often loses its significance in mere suggestiveness. His meaning is the burden of his story, not the automatic moral complement of its vivid and actual reality. Hence the sense of reality is absent from it, and for this nothing will atone in any form of art where the sense of unreality is not sought instead. It is rather singular that this latter effect is one he never sought. He never entered fairy-land—except to retell its classic tales in his manuals, "The Wonder Book" and "Tanglewood Tales."

His faculty of discovering morals on which tales could be framed is prodigious. It rises to the distinction of a special capacity of the mind, like the gift for languages or a genius for chess. It is, as one may say, a by-product of the Puritan preoccupation. He did not find sermons in stones. He had the sermons already; his task was to find the stones to fit them. And these his fancy furnished him with a fertility paralleling his use for them. But his interest in shaping these was concentrated on their illustrative and not on their real qualities. Instead of realizing vividly and presenting concretely the elements of his allegory, he contented himself with their plausibility as symbols. On this he always insisted and to compass it he expended much ingenuity. His fancy was of the kind that never completely looses its hold of the actual. His literary taste was too serious to content itself with pure mystification. The insubstantiality he sought was to consist in the envelope, not in the object. He desired to dissemble, not to abjure reality. But the sense of reality even as a substructure for fancifulness is not to be obtained merely by the ingenuity which finds a possible scientific basis for what performs its sole service as apparently imaginary.

To take a crude instance of this oftenest subtle practice: "Egotism, or the Bosom Serpent," is not, artistically speaking, made more real by the foot-note that explains the actual occurrence of the physical fact in several cases. The story *as a story* stands or falls by the reality with which the man with the snake in his bosom is presented. In the course of this presentation the victim exclaims, "It gnaws me! It gnaws me." "And then," the narrator says, "there was an audible hiss, but whether it came from the apparent lunatic's own lips, or was the real hiss of a serpent, might admit of discussion." We are, of course, spared the discussion, which might easily fail to interest us, but the point is that the suggestion of it is precisely one of those touches which diminish the sense of reality in the presentation, and of which Hawthorne is so inordinately fond. Here it is of small comparative importance. The same thing is even charming, I think, in the author's speculation about Donatello's possibly pointed ears in "The Marble Faun," though I think also that he greatly overworks his faun-like resemblance, which apparently he cannot convince himself he has made sufficiently clear, and follows to ridiculous lengths in Donatello's skippings and capriolings, as well as in his conformation and character. But oftenest his intrusion of symbolism, that parasite on allegory itself, is a crying abuse of a perfectly superficial and trivial expedient. He was, in fact, allegory-mad. . . . Consequently, he not only fails to handle the form in the minimizing manner of the masters, but often fails in effectiveness on the lower plane where the moral occupies the foreground. "The Birthmark" is an instance. . . .

In consequence, too, of this obsession by allegory, the tales in which he leaves it alone altogether, or at all events does not lean upon it, are the best, I think. His excellent faculty is released for freer play in such tales as "The Gentle Boy," in which, if he is less original, he is more human, and takes his place and holds his own in the lists of literature—instead of standing apart in the brown twilight and indulging his fancy in framing insubstantial fictions for the illustration of moral truths, not always of much moment. . . .

For the real misfortune of Hawthorne—and ours—was the misconception of his talent, resulting in this cultivation of his fancy to the neglect of his imagination. . . . And he neglected his imagination because he shrank from reality. Now, reality is precisely the province, the only province, the only concern, the only material of this noblest of faculties. It is, of course, as varied as the universe of which it is composed. There is the reality of "Tom Jones" and the reality of "Lear," for example; the reality of the ideal, indeed, as well as that of the phenomenal—its opposite being not the ideal but the fanciful. And Hawthorne coquetted and sported with it and made mirage of it. Instead of accepting it as the field of his imagination he made it the playground of his fancy.

Imagination and fancy differ, according to the old metaphysic, in that, both transcending experience, one observes and the other transgresses law. Everyone thus discriminates, at all events, between the imaginative and the fanciful. No writer ever had a deeper sense, or at least a firmer conviction, of the august immutability of law—those ordaining principles of the universe unbegotten by the race of mortal men and forever immune from the sleep of oblivion itself—to paraphrase the classic panegyric. His frequent theme—the soul and the conscience—absolutely implies the recognition of law and involves its acceptance. And philosophically his conception of his theme fundamentally, even fatalistically, insists on it. Three of the four novels embody its predetermination. But too often in his treatment of his theme its basis crumbles. The centre of gravity too often falls outside of it—falls outside of law as well as of experience— because reality impresses and appeals to him so little, because his necessity for dissolving it into the insubstantial is so imperative, that the theme itself is frittered away in the course of its exposition. The law, the moral truth, which is the point of departure, or, as I say, the foundation of his more serious work, is not only not enforced but positively enervated. At every turn the characters and events might, one feels, evade its constraint, so wholly do the unreal and the fantastic predominate in both their constitution and their evolution. Beings so insubstantial and transactions so fantastic (one or both elements are generally present), can but fitfully or feebly illustrate anything so solid and stable as the moral principles upon which the real universe is conducted.

From "Hawthorne," *Scribner's Magazine*, 43 (January 1908), 69-84.

VERNON LOUIS PARRINGTON

COOL, DETACHED, rationalistic, curiously inquisitive, he looked out upon the ferment of the times, the clash of rival philosophies and rival interests, only to bring them into his study and turn upon them the light of his critical analysis. One after another he weighed the several faiths of New England, conservative and transcendental and radical, and ended skeptic. . . . The universe in which he found himself was a moral universe, Hawthorne on the whole believed; and if that were true then man's chief business and urgent problem was the matter of a sufficient morality.

Radical in his intellectual processes, he could never become greatly interested in specific radicalisms. He is often thought of as a transcendentalist, and his association with the Peabodys and his venture into Brook Farm might seem to lend color to such an interpretation. Yet nothing in his intellectual sympathies marks him as of the school. The polar conceptions of transcendentalism repelled rather than attracted him. Political and metaphysical speculation left him cold, and the twin revolutionary forces of the time, French romanticism and German idealism, never deeply affected his thinking. Amid all the flux he retained much of the older Calvinist view of life and human destiny. Though nominally a Unitarian he did not share Channing's faith in the perfectibility of man. The buried voice of God that the transcendentalists professed to have discovered in instinct, he greatly distrusted. Man seemed to him quite as likely to turn out to be a child of the devil as the first-born of God. Perhaps through a long and uncertain process he may grow into something nobler than he now is, but for the present the fact remains that the human heart, if not desperately wicked, is at least on familiar terms with evil; too often it is cold, selfish, malignant, and its secret promptings need watching. Doubting the indwelling presence of the divine Over-soul, he could find no justification for the transcendental faith in the excellence of the universe, out of which came the genial optimism of the Emersonians. Too pronounced a rationalist to comprehend the mysticism that lurked in the heart of the transcendental faith, he remained cold to the revolutionary criticism that was eager to pull down the old temples to make room for nobler. Eager souls, mystics and revolutionaries, may propose to refashion the world in accordance with their dreams; but evil remains, and so long as it lurks in the secret places of the heart, Utopia is only the shadow of a dream. And so while the Concord thinkers were proclaiming man to be the indubitable child of God, Hawthorne was critically examining the question of evil as it appeared in the light of his own experience. It was the central, fascinating problem of his intellectual life, and in pursuit of a solution he probed curiously into the hidden, furtive recesses of the soul. . . .

Only in a narrow and very special sense was Hawthorne a romantic. With the romance of love and adventure he was never concerned; what interested him was the romance of ethics—the distortions of the soul under the tyranny of a diseased imagination. . . . Materials for romance were lying all about the Salem wharves—such a show of canvas and spars and rigging, such briny smells, such suggestions of far voyages to outlandish places, such strange figures slipping in from the ends of the earth. . . . A romantic could scarcely have found in America a setting better calculated to awaken a sense of brave adventure than in old Salem; yet for three years Hawthorne sat in the Custom House, with such materials all about him, and then turned away to the seventeenth century to write of Hester Prynne. . . .

This temperamental aloofness from objective reality was both the strength and the weakness of Hawthorne's art. In choosing to follow the way of the inner life he was true to his Puritan breeding. The perpetual turning-in of the mind upon itself, the long introspective brooding over human motives, came naturally to one who lived in the shadow of a Puritan past. In their anxious concern over sin the Puritans had become in some measure psychologists; how else could the secret impulses of the soul be probed and its dark workings laid bare? Hawthorne was only . . . examining the reactions of sin on conscience and character. From this comes the simplicity of his theme and the compelling unity of his handling. . . .

From the grave difficulties inherent in his theme [of imagined Puritanism and sin] came the inveterate habit of sliding into symbolism and allegory—from this and from the narrowness of his emotional life and the restrictions of his sympathies. The cold thin atmosphere of his work, one comes increasingly to feel, was due not alone or chiefly to the severity of his artistic restraint that forbade all rioting of the sensuous imagination; it was due rather to a lack of nourishment, to a poverty of ideas and sensuous imagery. His inveterate skepticism robbed him of much, but his inhibitions robbed him of more. A romantic uninterested in adventure and afraid of sex is likely to become somewhat graveled for matter. Like the Pyncheon fowls, Hawthorne's imagination had suffered from too long inbreeding; it had grown anemic, and every grain of fancy is clucked over and picked at and made much of. Once an idea comes into his head he is loath to let it go, but he must turn it about curiously and examine it from every angle. . . .

He was the extreme and finest expression of the refined alienation from reality that in the end palsied the creative mind of New England. Having consumed his fancies, what remained to feed on?

From *Main Currents in American Thought, Vol. II: The Romantic Revolution in America* (New York: Harcourt, Brace, 1927), pp. 442-50.

CONSTANCE ROURKE

HAWTHORNE, like Poe, was a writer who would naturally have worked best within a thoroughly established tradition; his predilections are shown in his care for style as well as by his choice of themes that were at least partially worked over and defined. His natural inclinations seem to have been toward comedy; his notebooks provide a singular contrast with his tales. They contain, it is true, many notes outlining poetical or abstract themes: but side by side with these are acute linear sketches of individuals, of groups, caught with immediacy and the fresh daylight upon them, seen with no veil of distance or of time. Throughout most of his years Hawthorne was on the outlook for odd and salient characters; he often enveloped them with humor in his brief notes; he had a gift for slight inflation in drawing, and even for the touch of caricature. From his boyhood at Salem when he was near the wharves with their changing crew of seafaring men, he had seen something of the rough fabric of a common and immediate life. As a youth at Bowdoin he had been on the fringe of the eastern backwoods with its inevitable small filtration of adventurers. Even in later years he betrayed a tie with this popular and common and often comic existence by his alliance with the invincible Peter Parley.

But that uncouth, unassimilated life about him, those casual aggregations of seamen and day-laborers and vagabonds—what after all did he know of them? His ignorance was not his alone: what did any one of his time know of them? Even his brief notes were adventures in recognition. Close elements of the native character had remained unstudied except for scattered and casual sketches, outlined mainly by unconcerned travelers impressed for the moment. Only prototypal drawings existed, of a few of the larger figures in American life, and in Hawthorne's formative years these provided no rich accumulation upon which to draw, which he might use for intensification.

Hawthorne turned toward a form which comedy more than any other native impulse was shaping within the popular consciousness, that of legend, which permitted a fantastic or narrow or generalized handling of character. The materials which he found were not comic; the older and more deeply established lore of New England was darkly tinged; his tales reveal a gamut of the more violent or terrible feelings, rage, terror, the sense of guilt, greed, strange regional fantasies, like that in *Ethan Brand,* witchcraft, ghosts. The scarlet letter was said to glow in the dark; Hawthorne suggested that the tale had come to him as lore; certainly much of *The House of the Seven Gables* came to him as tradition. In such works as *The Wonder Book* and *Tanglewood Tales* he again found the remote and legendary.

Even when his narratives were lengthened their scope was the brief scope of the tale; and though they did not join in cycles the tales were loosely linked. In his preface to *The House of the Seven Gables* Hawthorne disclaimed the purpose to write a novel, declaring that "the latter form of composition is presumed to aim at a very minute fidelity, not merely to the possible, but to the probable and ordinary course of man's experience." He called his narrative a romance, and insisted upon the right to mingle "the Marvellous" in its course, even though this might be only as "a slight, delicate, and evanescent flavor." Again, he spoke of the story as "a legend . . . from an epoch now gray in the distance . . . and bringing with it some of its legendary mist." Writing of some scenes from *The Scarlet Letter* which had been performed as an opera in New York, he said, "I should think it might possibly succeed as an opera, though it would certainly fail as a play." *The Scarlet Letter* had indeed the bold and poetic and legendary outline which may belong to opera; and the same qualities inhered in all of Hawthorne's finer work.

Though he drew upon a traditional material, Hawthorne could not rest at ease as the great English poets have rested within the poetic tradition that came to them through the ballads and romances, or as the great English novelists have drawn upon rich local accumulations of character and lore. The materials at his hand were not rich or dense or voluminous: time had not enriched but had scattered them. The effort to create imaginative writing out of such a groundwork must inevitably have been disruptive for an artist like Hawthorne; it was making bricks with only wisps of straw. The scantness of his natural sources may account for the meagerness of his effort, rather than some obscure inner maladjustment of his own; indeed, for a highly sensitive and traditional writer the constantly thwarted search for a richly established material could have caused a fundamental disarrangement of creative energy.

Yet if the result was small, Hawthorne's writing had freshness of accomplishment. In *The Scarlet Letter* a woman was drawn as a full and living figure for the first time in American literature. The semblance of a society was depicted; the Puritan settlement becomes a protagonist in the tale. This attempt toward a new and difficult portrayal was still slight and partial; the society appears mainly as a mob under strong emotion; and in *The House of the Seven Gables,* where a small group is imaged, its members filter one by one out of the shop door or are mentioned from a distance. Hawthorne entered an even more difficult area. In *The Scarlet Letter,* for the first time in an American narrative, emotion played a prevailing and simple part, restrained though it was by barriers which seemed persistently set against the expression of deep feeling. There can be no doubt of the love that existed between Dimmesdale and Hester; yet this is never expressed in a word, scarcely by a sign: it is shown only by a kind of running emotional shorthand in their brief exchanges. Their meeting in the wood was the first scene created by the American imagination in which emotion is all but overwhelming; some may call it the single great scene in American literature where love is dominant: but even here there is no direct revelation.

Hawthorne was deeply engaged by the consideration of lost or submerged emotion. In *The Scarlet Letter* this makes the basic theme: it was Dimmesdale's concealment of the bond with Hester which appears as his great wrong. It was warmth of affection, mingled with grief, which at last gave humanity to the elfin Pearl. Again and again in Hawthorne's briefer tales—sometimes only by allusion—he makes clear his conviction that the sin against the heart is the unpardonable sin. That suppression of individualized feeling, conspicuous in the American temper, was in a sense his major subject. Yet except in the one instance he seemed unable to reveal a deeply felt and simple emotion. The feelings which Hawthorne portrayed were for the most part complex or distorted; they were indeed, as in the writings of Poe, and in the romantic tragedy abroad in this period, mirrorings of those harsher feelings which had often belonged to a pioneer existence.

But these—rage, greed, terror, the sense of guilt—are only half lighted in Hawthorne's writing; they no longer take on the full fury which they had exercised on the frontier. He too plumbed the inner mind; he too was concerned with "introversion." For the most part his discoveries appeared in terms of pure fantasy; Hawthorne even transmuted regional legends into inner moods. Again and again in *The Scarlet Letter* the flow of the tale seems sensitively adapted to the flow of inner and secret feelings. In the passage describing the minister's impulses as he passes among his people after the meeting with Hester in the wood, Hawthorne reached a final and even prophetic discernment: here was a brief and effortless exposure of a grotesque inner license. Poe may have surpassed him in the discernment of subtle thoughts or impulses or in the definition of these: but Hawthorne portrayed the natural movement of a mind in a form which was to develop in modern literature, as direct revelation. No doubt Puritan influences created something of the bent toward inner scrutiny in Hawthorne. The Puritan element of judgment was often clear in his writings, though, as he said, it was sometimes deliberately added. But Hawthorne at his finest never used the abstract formulations of the Puritan: he chose the direct and earthy mode, as in the passage on Dimmesdale's fantasies: and there at least he slipped into an irreverent rude comedy far from the conscious Puritan habit. With all the delicacy of his approach, with all the invention which fairly transformed style into a means of revealing phases of buried thought or feeling, Hawthorne like Poe was close to the rude fantasy-making of the pioneer.

From *American Humor: A Study of the National Character* (New York: Harcourt, Brace, 1931), pp. 186-91.

YVOR WINTERS

IT IS noteworthy that in this passage from *The Scarlet Letter* [where Hester's scarlet A is disproportionately mirrored in the suit of armor, an ironic emblem of brute strength and simple directness among the ancestral portraits in Puritan Governor Bellingham's house] Hawthorne turns his instrument of allegory, the gift of the Puritans, against the Puritans themselves, in order to indicate the limits of their intelligence; it is noteworthy also that this act of criticism, though both clear and sound, is negative, that he nowhere except in the very general notion of regeneration through repentance establishes the nature of the intelligence which might exceed the intelligence of the Puritans, but rather hints at the ideal existence of a richer and more detailed understanding than the Puritan scheme of life is able to contain. The strength of *The Scarlet Letter* is in part safe-guarded by the refusal to explore this understanding; the man who was able in the same lifetime to write *The New Adam and Eve*, to conceive the art-colony described in *The Marble Faun*, and to be shocked at the nude statues of antiquity, was scarcely the man to cast a clear and steady light upon the finer details of the soul.

The conception of the book in general is as cleanly allegorical as is the conception of the passage quoted. Hester represents the repentant sinner, Dimmesdale the half-repentant sinner, and Chillingworth the unrepentant sinner. The fact that Chillingworth's sin is the passion for revenge is significant only to the extent that this is perhaps the one passion which most completely isolates man from normal human sympathies and which therefore is most properly used to represent an unregenerate condition.

The method of allegorization is that of the Puritans themselves; the substance of the allegory remained in a crude form a part of their practical Christianity in spite of their Calvinism, just as it remained in their non-theological linguistic forms, just as we can see it in the language of the best poems of so purely and mystically Calvinistic a writer as Jones Very, a living language related to a living experience, but overflowing the limits of Calvinistic dogma; Hawthorne's point of view was naturally more enlightened than that of the Puritans themselves, yet it was insufficiently so to enable him to recover the traditional Christian ethics except in the most general terms and by way of historical sympathy, for had a more complete recovery been possible, he would not have been so narrowly bound to the method of allegory and the frustration of the later romances would scarcely have been so complete.

Once Hawthorne had reduced the problem of sin to terms as general as these, and had brought his allegory to perfect literary form, he had, properly speaking, dealt with sin once and for all; there was nothing further to be said about it. It would not serve to write another allegory with a new set of characters and a different sin as the motive; for the particular sin is not particular in function, but is merely representative of sin in general, as the characters, whatever their names and conditions may be, are merely representative of the major stages of sin—there is no escape from the generality so long as one adheres to the method. There was nothing further, then, to be done in this direction, save the composition of a few footnotes to the subject in the form of sketches.

The only alternative remaining was to move away from the allegorical extreme of narrative toward the specific, that is, toward the art of the novelist. The attempt was made, but fell short of success. In *The House of the Seven Gables* and in *The Marble Faun* alike the moral understanding of the action—and there is a serious attempt at such understanding, at least in *The Marble Faun*—is corrupted by a provincial sentimentalism ethically far inferior to the Manicheism of the Puritans, which was plain and comprehensive, however brutal. And Hawthorne had small gift for the creation of human beings, a defect allied to his other defects and virtues: even the figures in *The Scarlet Letter* are unsatisfactory if one comes to the book expecting to find a novel, for they draw their life not from specific and familar [sic] human characteristics, as do the figures of Henry James, but from the precision and intensity with which they render their respective ideas; the very development of the story is neither narrative nor dramatic, but expository. When, as in *The Marble Faun* or *The House of the Seven Gables,* there is no idea governing the human figure, or when the idea is an incomplete or unsatisfactory equivalent of the figure, the figure is likely to be a disappointing spectacle, for he is seldom if ever a convincing human being and is likely to verge on the ludicrous. Hawthorne had not the rich and profound awareness of immediacy which might have saved a writer such as Melville in a similar predicament.

His effort to master the novelist's procedure, however, was not sustained, for his heart was not in it. In *The Blithedale Romance,* he began as a novelist, but lost himself toward the close in an unsuccessful effort to achieve allegory; the four unfinished romances represent similar efforts throughout. . . .

In *The Scarlet Letter* there occurs a formula which one might name the formula of alternative possibilities. [Mr. Winters quotes from chapter 9 the citizens' varied and unresolved arguments for their prejudice against Chillingworth and quotes from chapter 18 Hawthorne's conjectures about Pearl's relation to the forest and wild animals. He continues thus:] Similarly, in *The Marble Faun,* one never learns whether Donatello had or had not the pointed ears which serve throughout the book as the physical symbol of his moral nature; the book ends with the question being put to Kenyon, who has had opportunities to observe, and with his refusing to reply.

This device, though it becomes a minor cause of irritation through constant recurrence, is relatively harmless, and at times is even used with good effect. If we reverse the formula, however, so as to make the physical representation perfectly clear but the meaning uncertain, we have a very serious situation; and this is precisely what occurs, in some measure toward the close of *The Blithedale Romance*, and without mitigation throughout the four unfinished romances. We have in the last all of the machinery and all of the mannerisms of the allegorist, but we cannot discover the substance of his communication, nor is he himself aware of it so far as we can judge. We have the symbolic footprint, the symbolic spider, the symbolic elixirs and poisons, but we have not that of which they are symbolic; we have the hushed, the tense and confidential manner, on the part of the narrator, of one who imparts a grave secret, but the words are inaudible. Yet we have not, on the other hand, anything approaching realistic fiction, for the events are improbable or even impossible, and the characters lack all reality. The technique neither of the novelist nor of the allegorist was available to Hawthorne when he approached the conditions of his own experience: he had looked for signals in nature so long and so intently, and his ancestors before him had done so for so many generations, that, like a man hypnotized, or like a man corroded with madness, he saw them; but he no longer had any way of determining their significance, and he had small talent for rendering their physical presence with intensity. . . .

In *The Scarlet Letter*, then, Hawthorne composed a great allegory; or, if we look first at the allegorical view of life upon which early Puritan society was based, we might almost say that he composed a great historical novel. History, which by placing him in an anti-intellectual age had cut him off from the ideas which might have enabled him to deal with his own period, in part made up for the injustice by facilitating his entrance, for a brief time, into an age more congenial to his nature. Had he possessed the capacity for criticizing and organizing conceptions as well as for dramatizing them, he might have risen superior to his disadvantages, but like many other men of major genius he lacked this capacity. In turning his back upon the excessively simplified conceptions of his Puritan ancestors, he abandoned the only orderly concepts, whatever their limitations, to which he had access, and in his last work he is restless and dissatisfied. . . . His dilemma, the choice between abstractions inadequate or irrelevant to experience on the one hand, and experience on the other as far as practicable unilluminated by understanding, is tragically characteristic of the history of this country and of its literature. . . .

From *Maule's Curse: Seven Studies in the History of American Obscurantism* (Norfolk, Conn.: New Directions, 1938), pp. 15-22.

CHARLES FEIDELSON, JR.

WHILE HE stated clearly enough that he sought to mediate between the private vision and the common-sense objective world, he was likely at the same time, adopting an apologetic tone, to speak of his work as "fancy-pictures" and "castles in the air," as though his aim were simply the amusement of cutting himself loose from any reality.

The natural outcome of this theoretical indecisiveness was Hawthorne's allegorical method; by this means, consciously or not, he evaded the issue with which he was confronted. For it is in the nature of allegory, as opposed to symbolism, to beg the question of absolute reality. The allegorist avails himself of a formal correspondence between "ideas" and "things," both of which he assumes as given; he need not inquire whether either sphere is "real" or whether, in the final analysis, reality consists in their interaction. Hawthorne's initial notes for his tales are for the most part abstract formulas, equally remote from the subjective and the objective world: "Personify the Century—talk of its present middle-age—of its youth, and its adventures—of its prospects." Such schemata point to a parallelism between the two worlds, but hardly would lead to richness either of imagination or of physical substance, and certainly would never produce a meeting in which each might "imbue itself with the nature of the other." If Hawthorne's writings tend to be thin in both respects, it is because he never fully faced the problem of knowledge which his own situation raised.

Yet his underlying purpose was always "to open an intercourse with the world," and out of this purpose arose not allegory but symbolism. The "Custom House" essay, introductory to *The Scarlet Letter,* is a portrait of the artist as symbolist in spite of himself. Of course Hawthorne indulges in his usual *peccavi:* "It was a folly, with the materiality of this daily life pressing so intrusively upon me, to attempt to fling myself back into another age; or to insist on creating the semblance of a world out of airy matter. . . . The fault was mine." But this reverence for the material present and trivial view of the imagination do not obscure the central theme of the sketch—the theme implicit in the vignette of Hawthorne poring over the scarlet letter. That self-portrait—which, be it noted, is a self-projection, since Hawthorne in point of fact came upon his subject quite otherwise—amounts to a dramatic definition of the following "romance" and of the author's relation to it. The author's *donnée,* as James would call it, is neither Imagination nor Actuality per se but a symbol whose inherent meaning is *The Scarlet Letter.* The world that the writer seeks is generated by contemplation of the symbol, not by the external yoking-together of two realms which by definition are different in kind. This integral act of perception effectually "opens" an imaginative reality. That it is not the material reality of nineteenth-century Salem becomes wholly irrelevant, since the meaning of the symbol, accreted by generations who have lived with it and in it, is continuous in time.

Such would seem to be the implication of the essay as a whole. The Custom House itself, with Hawthorne as Surveyor of the Customs, is the stage for potential commerce or "intercourse with the world." The Custom House is at once the Surveyor's ally and his enemy. As enemy, it destroys his creative power by involving him in material commerce, in weighing and gauging, in all the mechanistic ways of thinking which, as Melville said, make "the round world itself but an empty cipher, except to sell by the cartload." On the other hand, business at the Salem wharf is virtually at a standstill, and the Custom House actually imposes very few practical duties on the Surveyor. As his ally, it embodies, like its aged inhabitants, the residue of past experience; it is the analogue of the Surveyor's own consciousness, in which, though a mere "writer of storybooks," he feels a continuity with his Puritan and seafaring ancestors. Thus the Custom House makes possible another kind of commerce and another kind of revenue: a traffic with the world by means of the significance vested in a traditional symbol. The discovery of the scarlet letter amid the old documents of the Customs—lists of wrecked or rotten ships and dead merchants—signalizes not a retreat into the past but a penetration into persistent meaning.

In this way "The Custom House" throws light on a theme in *The Scarlet Letter* which is easily overlooked amid the ethical concerns of the book. Every character, in effect, re-enacts the "Custom House" scene in which Hawthorne himself contemplated the letter, so that the entire "romance" becomes a kind of exposition of the nature of symbolic perception. Hawthorne's subject is not only the meaning of adultery but also meaning in general; not only *what* the focal symbol means but also *how* it gains significance. This aspect of the book is emphasized by Hawthorne's pointed use of the most problematic kind of symbol, a letter, and by his method of circling interpretation through the minds of various characters. . . .

The truth is that symbolism at once fascinated and horrified him. While it spoke to his "sensibilities," it evaded "the analysis of [his] mind." On the one hand, the symbol was valuable precisely because it transcended analytic thought; on the other hand, that very transcendence, with its suggestion of the unconventional, the novel, the disorderly, was potentially dangerous. The letter had "deep meaning," but the letter was scarlet, and Pearl, its embodiment, had no "principle of being" save "the freedom of a broken law." Hawthorne dwells on the elusiveness, the rationally indefinable quality of Pearl, who "could not be made amenable to rules, . . . whose elements were perhaps beautiful and brilliant, but all in disorder; or with an order peculiar to themselves, amidst which the point of variety and arrangement was difficult or impossible to be discovered." Allegory was the brake that Hawthorne applied to his sensibility.

For allegory *was* analytic: allegory was safe because it preserved the conventional distinction between thought and things and because it depended on a conventional order whose point of arrangement was easily defined. The symbolistic and the allegorical patterns in Hawthorne's books reach quite different conclusions; or, rather, the symbolism leads to an inconclusive luxuriance of meaning, while allegory imposes the pat moral and the simplified character. This predicament comes to the surface in an absurd conversation between Kenyon and Miriam toward the end of *The Marble Faun*. Since Donatello has been symbolically identified with the statue of the Faun, in which "the characteristics of the brute creation meet and combine with those of humanity," his crime, from this point of view, is a necessary step in his attainment of fully human qualities. At the same time, Donatello has been associated with Adam, and his crime with the Fall of Man. The combination of these two meanings in the one character forces a reinterpretation of orthodox Evil. "Was the crime," Miriam asks, "in which he and I were wedded—was it a blessing, in that strange disguise?" This is more than Kenyon can stomach: "You stir up deep and perilous matter, Miriam. . . . I dare not follow you into the unfathomable abysses whither you are tending. . . . It is too dangerous." And Hawthorne himself repudiates "these meditations, which the sculptor rightly felt to be so perilous." He falls back on the simple morality of Hilda, a purely allegorical creature equipped with white robe, tower, lamp, and doves.

Yet there can be no doubt that Hawthorne experienced the attraction of inverted values—the extreme form of that anticonventional impulse which is inherent in symbolism. In the Roman Eden, he ventures to say, "the final charm is bestowed by the malaria. . . . For if you come hither in summer, and stray through these glades in the golden sunset, fever walks arm in arm with you, and death awaits you at the end of the dim vista." The "piercing, thrilling, delicious kind of regret" which these thoughts arouse in him points in an obvious direction: "Aux objets répugnants nous trouvons des appas." Baudelaire stood at the end of the dim vista. If Hawthorne was unduly anxious about the freedom of symbolic meaning, it may be to his credit that he had some inkling of how far that method could go.

From *Symbolism and American Literature* (Chicago: Univ. of Chicago Press, 1953), pp. 8-10, 14-16.

RICHARD HARTER FOGLE

THE LIGHT in Hawthorne is clarity of design. He has a classic balance; his language is exquisitely lucid. He gives one the sense of an invulnerable dignity and centrality; he is impenetrably self-possessed. He holds his characters to the highest standards, for he literally brings them to judgment at the bar of eternity as immortal souls. The "dark" in Hawthorne, that blackness which Herman Melville applauded in him, is his tragic complexity. His clarity is intermingled with subtlety, his statement interfused with symbolism, his affirmation enriched with ambiguity. The whole which results is captivating. In attack he is mild but deadly. His blow is so delicately delivered that a man would have to turn his head in order to realize that he had just lost it. "The Custom House" essay, for example, which rather oddly precedes *The Scarlet Letter,* seems at first sight merely agreeable. Look closer, however, and the effect is devastating. These gently humorous character portraits are murderous, not from malice or heat, but from judgment and icy cold. Hawthorne is not indignant; he is merely certain of his grounds. And his certainty is that of one whose father was called "the sternest man who ever walked a deck." . . .

The philosophy of Hawthorne is a broadly Christian scheme which contains heaven, earth, and hell. Whether heaven and hell are realities or only subjective states of mind is one of Hawthorne's crucial ambiguities. I do not call him a Christian humanist, as do some excellent critics, for it seems to me that heaven and hell *are* real to him and play too large a part in his fiction to be relegated to the background. In his mixed macrocosm, man is a microcosm also mixed. Man's chief temptation is to forget his limits and complexities, to think himself all good, or to think himself all bad. Either way he falls into spiritual isolation and pride. He needs a proper mixture of the earthly and the ideal—with a touch of the flame to temper it. Thus Aylmer, the scientist-hero of "The Birthmark," violates the covenant of humankind when he tries to eradicate the only blemish of his beautiful wife, a tiny mark on her cheek. He succeeds, but kills her in the process. The birthmark, which is shaped like a hand, is her grip upon earthly existence. She dies to the sound of the laughter of Aminadab, Aylmer's assistant, a kind of earth-fiend. Even the pit has its claims, which must not be slighted. . . .

Hawthorne still suffers from our prejudice against allegory. This prejudice comes partly from a false theory of realism, a legacy of the late nineteenth century, and partly from a misconception of what allegory is. We assume that allegory subordinates everything to a predetermined conclusion: that allegory, in short, is a dishonest counterfeit of literary value. But the great allegories, *The Faerie Queene* and *The Pilgrim's Progress,* possess the literary virtues. And Hawthorne, whose subjects are moral and psychological problems, feels for these problems a passion which transfigures them. All we can ask of a writer is that he treat his material honestly, without unduly simplifying: that he keep faith with his own imagination. T. S. Eliot has said that good religious poetry teaches us not a doctrine but how it feels to believe it; and so it should be with allegory.

Allegory is organic to Hawthorne, an innate quality of his vision. It is his disposition to find spiritual meaning in all things natural and human. This faculty is an inheritance from the Puritans, who saw in everything God's will. To this inheritance was added a gift from nineteenth-century Romanticism, which endowed the natural world with meaning by seeing it as life. In Hawthorne allegory is inseparable from moral complexity and aesthetic design, qualities to be enjoyed in themselves. . . .

Yvor Winters and F. O. Matthiessen have illuminated Hawthorne's ambiguity, which Winters calls "the formula of alternative possibilities," and Matthiessen "the device of multiple choice." It is not, however, a device; it is a pervasive quality of mind. It can be an evasion, and it is sometimes no more than a mannerism. But as a whole it embodies Hawthorne's deepest insights. It outlines the pure form of truth by dissolving irrelevancies; this is its positive function. Negatively, it marks the limit of eyeshot, beyond which is shadow. Thus Hawthorne's effects of light—his shadows, his mirror images, his masquerades—all examine the relationships of appearance and reality. Hawthorne's ambiguity involves both light and darkness. As light it is the means of seeing through opacities; as darkness it is the difficulty of seeing. . . .

The issues [compared to those of *A Wonder-Book* and *Tanglewood Tales*] are more serious in such legends of New England as "The Gray Champion" and the "Legends of the Province House" in the volume of *Twice-Told Tales.* In these stories the ambiguity underlines the significance by dissolving irrelevant actuality in the mists of the past and leaving only an ideal history. Ambiguity invests the events with the rich pathos and patina of time and counterpoints unreality against truth. In "The Gray Champion" the hero's background is shadowed, the better to project his image in the foreground. In "Howe's Masquerade" disguise reveals identity; the procession of royal governors is a masquerade, but there is nothing false about its meaning. The ambiguity of the "Legends" is a vision of the Past in the light of the Present, a picture in a frame of distance.

Hawthorne uses ambiguity structurally to create suspense and retard conclusions, especially in tales where the primary emphasis would otherwise be too clear. "The Celestial Railroad," an ironic nineteenth-century *Pilgrim's Progress,* is an example of this usage. Hawthorne's railroad is scheduled to the Celestial City, but its real destination is Hell. By disguising the way to Perdition as the road to Heaven, he takes the reader into his confidence by a sustained ironic reversal of values and curbs impatience for the end by supplying attractions on the way. "The Celestial Railroad," however, is closer to abstract allegory than Hawthorne generally gets. More fundamental is the tragic ambiguity which threatens the bases of accepted values, as in "Young Goodman Brown," where the final interpretation is in genuine doubt. Hawthorne judges relentlessly, yet with sympathy, and his ambiguity always leaves room for a different verdict. He preserves the sanctity and independence of his characters by allowing them at bottom an inviolable individuality.

In their recently published *Theory of Literature,* Rene Wellek and Austin Warren define the symbol as "an object which refers to another object but which demands attention also in its own right, as a presentation." The symbol must be interesting in itself, not merely as it points to something else. This crucial requirement, which divides *mere* allegory from literature, Hawthorne fulfills. The minister's black veil is truly a veil, as well as an emblem of secret sin. The brook of *The Scarlet Letter* has water in it, though it symbolizes life and time. The fountain in Rappaccini's garden is an object of art in addition to being an image of eternity. Hawthorne's symbols have the clarity of allegory, with the complexity and density of life. They are rarely obscure, but they will abide the test of long use without wearing out. Since they are generally accompanied by an explanation, it is natural to pass by them quickly—too quickly.

The rosebush before the prison in Chapter I of *The Scarlet Letter* is an instance of this misleading simplicity. It stands, says Hawthorne, "in token that the deep heart of nature can pity and forgive." The rose is pitying nature, as the prison is pitiless man. The rose is also, however, Hester Prynne, a red rose against the gray Puritan background; and therefore it is the scarlet letter, the natural passion which the prison exists to quell. Beside the fortress-like prison the rose seems pitiably frail, but it is strong with the power of natural vitality.

Hawthorne's symbols are broadly traditional, drawn from the main stream of Western thought. In his pages are the red cavern of the heart and the gray cavern of isolation; the wild forest and the winding path of error (from Spenser); the fountain and the sea of eternity, and the river of time; the Garden of Eden, with Adam and Eve and the serpent; the flames of hell, strangely mingled with the forge fire of Vulcan's smithy, and the bright blaze of the hearth; the devil's stigmata, and the sunlight of holiness. Created as they are of old materials, these symbols are yet fresh from Hawthorne's imagination. He invests them with a new vitality and suggestiveness.

From *Hawthorne's Fiction: The Light & the Dark* (1952; rev. Norman: Univ. of Oklahoma Press, 1964), pp. 4-7, 11-14.

Critical Essays

RICHARD P. ADAMS

Hawthorne's *Provincial Tales*

[HAWTHORNE'S early projected *Provincial Tales*] all have essentially the same theme: the transition from childishness or adolescence to maturity. They are all historical in their settings and in the specific terms of their presentation. And although they approach their mutual theme from different directions, making for a surface variety of treatment, they overlap in many ways, so that even the surface treatment is fairly homogeneous. In general "Young Goodman Brown" illustrates a moral approach, "The Maypole of Merry Mount" an esthetic approach, "My Kinsman, Major Molineux" a sociological approach, "The Gray Champion" a political approach, "Roger Malvin's Burial" a psychological approach, and "The Gentle Boy" a religious approach. But there is a strong esthetic flavor to the religious controversy that motivates "The Gentle Boy," and that controversy has political implications too. The political conflict in "The Gray Champion" also involves a religious quarrel and some strong esthetic differences; and these three aspects are also present in "The Maypole of Merry Mount." "My Kinsman, Major Molineux" combines political and psychological aspects with its primarily sociological treatment, and "Young Goodman Brown" contains in its extremely complex unity almost everything that the group as a whole represents. . . .

"Young Goodman Brown" is generally considered the best of the *Provincial Tales* and one of the best stories Hawthorne ever wrote. It is also important because it contains the germ of nearly all his best work to follow. It would be at least partly true to say that *The Scarlet Letter* or *The Marble Faun* is only "Young Goodman Brown" grown older and bigger.

The question of maturity for Goodman Brown is put in terms of good and evil. At first it seems a fairly simple choice, but the problem is much more complex than Brown seems ever to realize. He leaves the daylit street of Salem Village, saying goodbye to his wife, Faith, with pink ribbons in her cap, and goes into the darkening forest. There, by appointment, he meets the devil, who tries to persuade him to attend a witch meeting, saying that his father and grandfather have often done so and that the leaders of the Puritan community are generally in attendance. Brown, making his simple choice of good over evil, refuses. His confidence is somewhat shaken when they see old Goody Cloyse on the path ahead and he learns that she, who has taught him his catechism, is on her way to the meeting. But he still refuses, and the devil leaves him. As he is congratulating himself on his moral purity and fortitude, he is further disconcerted by hearing the minister and Deacon Gookin riding through the forest on the same errand. His resolution is broken when a heavy cloud goes over and he hears the voices of people he knows in Salem, including that of his wife. He shouts her name, she screams, and one of her pink ribbons flutters down. At this Brown rejects the good he has chosen and embraces evil, rushing through the forest after the devil, himself more like a devil than a man, until he comes to the firelit clearing where the witch meeting is being held.

In the meeting, especially its setting, evil is associated so closely as practically to identify it with sex. At the end of the clearing is a rock used as an altar or pulpit, "surrounded by four blazing pines, their tops aflame, their stems untouched, like candles at an evening meeting. The mass of foliage that had overgrown the summit of the rock was all on fire. . . . " The imagery of fire is typically used by Hawthorne, both before and after the *Provincial Tales,* to connote intense emotion, especially sexual passion, which is specified if anything too obviously here by the physiological correspondences of the pines and the brush-covered rock. But, almost as often in Hawthorne, fire also connotes the warmth of personal and familial association, as opposed to the coldness of isolation. Brown's feelings as he approaches are accordingly mixed. He is surprised to see that the congregation includes many presumably virtuous people, as well as "men of dissolute lives and women of spotted fame," and he finds it "strange to see that the good shrank not from the wicked, nor were the sinners abashed by the saints." But as he steps out into the clearing he too feels the "loatheful brotherhood" between himself and the others "by the sympathy of all that was wicked in his heart." It might be more accurate to say by all that is sexual in his character. A parallel ambiguity is suggested by the fact that, as it seems to him, "the shape of his own dead father beckoned him to advance, looking downward from a smoke wreath, while a woman, with dim features of despair, threw out her hand to warn him back. Was it his mother?" If so, the two play typical roles, the father encouraging the son to become a man, the mother trying to keep him a child as long as possible.

Brown and Faith are led to the altar, where the devil, in the guise of a Puritan minister, proposes to reveal the " 'secret deeds' "—that is, the sexual crimes —of their neighbors. . . .

The prospect [of baptismal initiation into the mystery of sin] is too much for Brown, who at this point makes his final decision, rejects evil, and commands Faith to " 'look up to heaven, and resist the wicked one.' " Instantly the congregation, Faith, and the devil disappear, and Brown is alone, "amid calm night and solitude," while the foliage that has been blazing with fire now sprinkles him "with the coldest dew." He returns to Salem with his isolation around him like a cloak, shrinks away from the minister, wonders what god Deacon Gookin is praying to, snatches a child away from Goody Cloyse, and passes his wife, Faith, in the street without a word. Through the rest of his long life, Goodman Brown is "A stern, a sad, a darkly meditative, a distrustful, if not a desperate man. . . . "

The most immediately apparent reason for this final state of Brown's mind is that he has been required to face and acknowledge the evil in himself and others, including his young wife, so as to be able to recognize the good, and has failed the test. Having refused to look at evil, he is left in a state of moral uncertainty that is worse, in a way, than evil itself. His inability to judge between good and evil also prevents him from entering into stable social relations or having any sort of intimate contact with others. He has lost Faith, as he says at one point in the story, in all the ways that the ambiguities of the name can be made to mean. For Hawthorne, this condition of moral and social isolation is the worst evil that can befall a man.

But the more important aspect of Brown's personal disaster is his failure to grow up, in the sense of becoming emotionally mature. This is not itself a matter of good and evil, though it is a matter where good and evil are always potentially present. . . . In place of the needed capacity for both love and hate or, in the terms of the story, both evil and good, he develops only a great fear of moral maturity and of the knowledge and responsibility that maturity brings.

The other tales of the group throw different lights on the common theme by approaching it from their different points of view. "The Maypole of Merry Mount" poses a predominantly esthetic question against the background of a cultural conflict [between the gay Merry Mount colonists and the gloomy Puritans]. . . . Hawthorne, though hardly himself a frivolous person, would have welcomed a little more of the Maypole spirit than he found in the New England of his own time. He was partly in earnest too when he blamed its gloom, and the darkness of his own soul, on the Puritan heritage.

The action of "The Maypole of Merry Mount" is even simpler than that of "Young Goodman Brown." Edith and Edgar, on their wedding day, are forced by Endicott, the ironclad, iron-souled Puritan leader, to leave their formerly happy home at Merry Mount and take up life among the somber but eminently grown-up Puritans. Their transition (Edgar's more specifically) is not altogether easy, but it is what Hawthorne seems to regard as normal. We need not suppose he means that grown-ups all have to be Puritans, but he shows here and elsewhere a real admiration of certain Puritan qualities, such as moral strength and seriousness, courage, firmness, and determination. These are precisely the qualities of maturity that young Goodman Brown most conspicuously lacks. Edgar, by contrast and in spite of his youth in Merry Mount, has already gained some share of them. Therefore, encouraged by similar virtues in the character of Edith, he is able to impress the stern Endicott as being at least potentially fit for the adult society of Massachusetts Bay.

Much the same kind of transition is shown from the social point of view by what happens to Robin in "My Kinsman, Major Molineux." Having left his home in the hope of being advanced in the world by his rich and powerful kinsman, he is forced to renounce the kinsman and make his own way. The typical revolt of the son against the authority of the father is here related to some unidentified incident of revolt on the part of the Colony, or at any rate a large number of the Colonists, against the parent country or a symbol or representative of it in the person of the Major. Thus Robin's desertion of his family is associated with America's desertion of the British Empire.

The action of this tale is more complex than that of either "Young Goodman Brown" or "The Maypole of Merry Mount." Robin arrives in the provin-

cial metropolis (presumably Boston) late one evening, tired and almost out of
money. The only resource he knows is to find his kinsman at once, but he is
unable to do so. When he inquires for the Major he is rebuffed, ridiculed,
insulted, threatened, and deceived, but nowhere able to learn anything helpful.
It becomes apparent to the reader, though not very clearly to Robin, that some
plot or agitation is on foot in which the Major is unpleasantly involved. Finally
Robin stops "a bulky stranger, muffled in a cloak," and demands information.
The stranger, baring his face, replies that the Major will pass by in an hour,
and Robin recognizes him as a man he has met earlier at an inn, impressive
for his bold features and eyes that "glowed . . . like fire in a cave." Now the
sight of him fills Robin with "dismay and astonishment" because one side of
his face blazes "an intense red" and the other is "black as midnight." "The
effect," says Hawthorne, "was as if two individual devils, a fiend of fire and
a fiend of darkness, had united themselves to form this infernal visage."

Robin, settling down to wait, imagines the scene at home, where his father
will be leading the family in outdoor prayer. But the fantasy ends with the door
of the house being shut in Robin's face. He is "excluded from his home." Thus
he takes the first step toward resolving his crisis by recognizing that he is cut
off from his immediate family, particularly his father. The results of this
recognition are first an intense feeling of loneliness and second a possibility
that he, like Edgar, may successfully complete the process of growing up.

Robin's loneliness is relieved toward the end of the hour when another
stranger comes along, a kindly citizen who listens to Robin's story and stays
to wait for the Major. Then a parade appears with the double devil at its head;
and in the midst, where the torches are brightest, sitting in tar and feathers
on a cart, is the Major, whose recognition of Robin seems to be his crowning
indignity. "They stared at each other in silence, and Robin's knees shook, and
his hair bristled, with a mixture of pity and terror." His catharsis is completed
when he recognizes all the various people he has met during the evening and
joins with them in the monstrous laugh that goes up; and by so doing he
completes his declaration of independence by repudiating the father-substitute
embodied in his kinsman and would-be sponsor. When the parade has moved
on, Robin thinks he will go back home, but the kindly citizen points out the
significance of his recent experience by suggesting that he stay in town and
remarking that " 'perhaps, as you are a shrewd youth, you may rise in the world
without the help of your kinsman, Major Molineux.' "

There is interest enough on the surface of this tale, which is a fine imaginative handling of a local uprising, the entanglement of a young man in affairs
beyond his comprehension, and his extrication from the difficulty, partly by
his own efforts and partly by the help of two men, one stern and the other
kindly. But this interest is multiplied by deeper meanings. The action is, in
one aspect, an initiation ceremony, marking and confirming the young man's
establishment of a new, mature set of relations with his family and with society.
The typical initiation test represents externally the psychological difficulties
involved in this process, and by externalizing them renders them easier to
surmount than they are when the boy has to wrestle with them privately, as

he usually does in our society. It is essentially this test that Goodman Brown fails.

Edgar, in "The Maypole of Merry Mount," passes it in much the same way as Robin. Edgar's real father is not mentioned, but he has a substitute in the Anglican priest who marries him to Edith. Endicott's function is first to force Edgar to renounce the priest as a father image and then encourage him to take his place as an adult among the Puritans. The suggestion of the public ritual element is strong in all three tales.

In "Roger Malvin's Burial," however, with its dominantly psychological approach, the public aspect is almost entirely absent. The privacy of the struggle and the difficulty of winning through the crisis are emphasized in this tale more than in any of the others, even "Young Goodman Brown." The basic problem is the same. Reuben Bourne, the protagonist, returning with Roger Malvin from Lovell's fight with the Indians, is forced to leave the badly wounded older man, after promising to come back or send a party to rescue or, as seems more likely, bury him. Reuben is prevented from carrying out this promise, first by his collapse from exhaustion and his own wounds, and then, when he has partly recovered, by a kind of moral cowardice which keeps him from admitting that he has not stayed with Malvin to the end. These circumstances are given added meaning and emotional force by two related facts. Malvin, in urging Reuben to leave him, says that he has loved him like a father and " 'should have something of a father's authority.' " And Reuben's most powerful motive for leaving, a motive which he fails to acknowledge even to himself, is that he wants to marry Malvin's daughter, Dorcas. Partly for these reasons, he is led to conceal the truth of the matter, most particularly from Dorcas.

This concealment, rather than anything wrong or disgraceful about the desertion itself, Hawthorne says "imparted to a justifiable act much of the secret effect of guilt," and it makes Reuben unable to protect himself from even more uncomfortable thoughts. "By a certain association of ideas, he at times almost imagined himself a murderer." The worst trial of all is that he is subject to "a haunting and torturing fancy that his father-in-law was yet sitting at the foot of the rock, on the withered forest leaves, alive, and awaiting his pledged assistance." Apparently there is nothing terribly wrong with leaving one's father, even though such a desertion seems in a way like murder. But leaving him unburied may be dangerous. As long as Malvin remains alive in Reuben's secret memory, Reuben cannot act the part of a man or be a proper father himself. He and Dorcas marry and have a son, Cyrus, so that physically Reuben is a father, as Goodman Brown is after his ordeal in the forest. But, like Brown, Reuben is emotionally or psychologically unable to accept the father's role. Instead he finds his only relief from the neurotic feelings that plague him by identifying himself with the dependent and therefore innocent boy, in whom "he recognized what he had himself been in other days." He is arrested in a childish attitude.

Reuben's neurotic indolence and contentiousness gradually reduce his fortunes to such a degree that, after eighteen years, he is forced to abandon the farm he has inherited from Malvin and go pioneering. Unconsciously he leads his family to the place where he has left Malvin, and there, in search of game, with his mind hovering on the verge of recognition, he fires at a movement in the bushes and kills his son. At that moment he realizes where he is, and when Dorcas comes he tells her that her father and her son lie dead together. Then the weight of the secret is removed, or, as Hawthorne puts it, "His sin was expiated,—the curse was gone from him; and in the hour when he had shed blood dearer to him than his own, a prayer, the first for years, went up to Heaven from the lips of Reuben Bourne." Logically, this ending makes no sense—indeed it makes badly perverted nonsense—but psychologically it has some interesting meanings.

The main point is that Reuben is able to free himself of dependence on Malvin only when he recognizes that his foster father is really dead and in effect buried, and when he ratifies that recognition by destroying the concrete equivalent of his childishness as he sees it in Cyrus. So interpreted, "Roger Malvin's Burial" is an allegory, more or less symbolic, of the same universal experience dealt with in the other stories in the group. But Reuben Bourne succeeds in surmounting the crisis of adolescence at a price that must make any reader feel uncomfortable, however puzzled he may be by the confusing terms in which the story is presented.

Ilbrahim, in "The Gentle Boy," does not succeed; he is persecuted to death at the age of about seven years because he insists on being a Quaker in the Puritan Colony. His father has been hanged. His mother has left him with foster parents who do the best they can for him but who fail in their efforts to bring him into their church and community and who cannot give him the kind of spiritual relations he needs. Because he is too young and weak to make his way, or to make the kind of impression on the Puritans that Edgar makes on Endicott in "The Maypole of Merry Mount," he is forced continually farther into isolation, until it ends in death.

"The Gray Champion" seems at first to have as its protagonist the old Puritan who emerges from the crowd and halts the governor and his soldiers, preventing a riot that might have become an earlier Boston Massacre. But a more logical protagonist, in view of the general theme of the group, is the Colony of Massachusetts Bay. It is the Colony that is immature but growing, that is straining the political and legal bonds of dependence on England, and that will eventually, with the other twelve, declare and establish its independence. The Gray Champion has the same function as the kindly citizen in "My Kinsman, Major Molineux": that of encouraging and helping the protagonist in his encounter with the devil-figure.

The common theme of the *Provincial Tales* is not basically a question of good versus evil, but rather of boyish dependence and carelessness versus manly freedom and responsibility. And it is very much a question of the protagonist's passing from the one state to the other or failing to do so—a question of time, change, and development. . . .

Even the typical structure of the *Provincial Tales* is dynamic. It consists of a pattern of three or four characters who move in a series of shifting relationships. The protagonist, a naive young man, is attracted by a woman, who somehow seems to bring him into conflict with an evil man or devil. Sometimes he is helped by a benevolent older man, more often not; but essentially the number of characters is always four because when only three appear the devil-figure has a double function. He both frightens and encourages the youthful candidate. This pattern can be most completely demonstrated in "My Kinsman, Major Molineux." Robin, after briefly meeting the devil-figure without makeup, is attracted by a young woman who pretends to be the Major's housekeeper and who evidently aims to seduce him. Then he meets the devil in full rig, and then the kindly citizen who confirms his maturity and encourages him to stay and make it good.

In the other tales the pattern is less complete, but its meanings are sometimes clearer. The function of the woman, for example, is much more plainly evident in "Roger Malvin's Burial" than it is in "My Kinsman, Major Molineux." Reuben sees Malvin as the friendly foster father until he marries Dorcas. Then Malvin haunts him until he declares himself mature, at which point Malvin again seems to be the benevolent father. . . .

We must remember that this is an abstract pattern, useful only insofar as it helps us to understand the stories. . . .

The most important values in the *Provincial Tales* are finally esthetic; . . . in Hawthorne's *Provincial Tales* we find the earliest creative work done and published in the United States in which the true positive romantic note is struck and held.

The best evidence in support of this claim is Hawthorne's dynamic use of the pattern of symbolic death and rebirth. . . .

The romantics make it [truth] dynamic. In works such as *Faust, The Ancient Mariner,* and *The Prelude* the pattern of death and rebirth ends, if it can be said to end at all, at a point beyond its beginning. It is not a matter of doubt and reconciliation, or an emotionally enriched return to a given formula. It involves the discovery of a new attitude which enables the protagonist to carry his revolt through to a sort of open completion; to make it, in fact, not just a revolt against an old truth but a radical departure from all old concepts of truth as a static value. The romantic protagonist dies in much the same symbolic sense as his humanistic predecessor, by withdrawing from the generally accepted ways of thinking and feeling. But he is reborn in a very different sense and into a whole new, different world. Instead of returning he goes on indefinitely. . . .

Hawthorne handles the romantic theme very well. His unresolved ambiguities express the conflicts out of which the romantic development comes, and mean something more than just the tough-minded acceptance of the fact that men are both good and evil. They strongly imply a transcendence of good and evil as absolute, static values or concepts, because it is out of the tension between these opposites that the power to move onward is generated. . . .

From "Hawthorne's *Provincial Tales*," *The New England Quarterly*, 30 (March 1957), 39-57.

D. H. LAWRENCE

Nathaniel Hawthorne
and "The Scarlet Letter"

THERE IS A basic hostility in all of us between the physical and the mental, the blood and the spirit. The mind is "ashamed" of the blood. And the blood is destroyed by the mind, actually. Hence pale-faces.

At present the mind-consciousness and the so-called spirit triumphs. In America supremely. In America, nobody does anything from the blood. Always from the nerves, if not from the mind. The blood is chemically reduced by the nerves, in American activity. . . .

For a long time men *believed* that they could be perfected through the mind, through the spirit. They believed, passionately. They had their ecstasy in pure consciousness. They *believed* in purity, chastity, and the wings of the spirit.

America soon plucked the bird of the spirit. America soon killed the *belief* in the spirit. But not the practice. The practice continued with a sarcastic vehemence. America, with a perfect inner contempt for the spirit and the consciousness of man, practises the same spirituality and universal love and KNOWING all the time, incessantly, like a drug habit. And inwardly gives not a fig for it. Only for the *sensation*. The pretty-pretty *sensation* of love, loving all the world. And the nice fluttering aeroplane *sensation* of knowing, knowing, knowing. Then the prettiest of all sensations, the sensation of UNDERSTAND-ING. Oh, what a lot they understand, the darlings! *So* good at the trick, they are. Just a trick of self-conceit.

The Scarlet Letter gives the show away.

You have your pure-pure young parson Dimmesdale.

You have the beautiful Puritan Hester at his feet.

And the first thing she does is to seduce him.

And the first thing he does is to be seduced.

And the second thing they do is to hug their sin in secret, and gloat over it, and try to understand.

Which is the myth of New England. . . .

Oh, Hester, you are a demon. A man *must* be pure, just that you can seduce him to a fall. Because the greatest thrill in life is to bring down the Sacred Saint with a flop into the mud. Then when you've brought him down, humbly wipe off the mud with your hair, another Magdalen. And then go home and dance a witch's jig of triumph, and stitch yourself a Scarlet Letter with gold thread, as duchesses used to stitch themselves coronets. And then stand meek on the scaffold and fool the world. Who will all be envying you your sin, and beating you because you've stolen an advantage over them. . . .

Look out, Mister, for the Female Devotee. Whatever you do, don't let her start tickling you. She knows your weak spot. Mind your Purity.

When Hester Prynne seduced Arthur Dimmesdale it was the beginning of the end. But from the beginning of the end to the end of the end is a hundred years or two.

Mr. Dimmesdale also wasn't at the end of his resources. Previously, he had lived by governing his body, ruling it, in the interests of his spirit. Now he has a good time all by himself torturing his body, whipping it, piercing it with thorns, macerating himself. It's a form of masturbation. He wants to get a mental grip on his body. And since he can't quite manage it with the mind, witness his fall—he will give it what for, with whips. His will shall *lash* his body. And he enjoys his pains. Wallows in them. To the pure all things are pure.

It is the old self-mutilation process, gone rotten. The mind wanting to get its teeth in the blood and flesh. The ego exulting in the tortures of the mutinous flesh. I, the ego, I *will* triumph over my own flesh. Lash! Lash! I am a grand free spirit. *Lash!* I am the master of my soul! *Lash! Lash!* I am the captain of my soul. *Lash!* Hurray! "In the fell clutch of circumstance," etc., etc.

Good-bye Arthur. He depended on women for his Spiritual Devotees, spiritual brides. So, the woman just touched him in his weak spot, his Achilles Heel of the flesh. Look out for the spiritual bride. She's after the weak spot. It is the battle of wills. . . .

A woman can use her sex in sheer malevolence and poison, while she is *behaving* as meek and good as gold. Dear darling, she is really snow-white in her blamelessness. And all the while she is using her sex as a she-devil, for the endless hurt of her man. She doesn't know it. She will never believe it if you tell her. And if you give her a slap in the face for her fiendishness, she will rush to the first magistrate, in indignation. She is so *absolutely* blameless, the she-devil, the dear, dutiful creature.

Give her the great slap, just the same, just when she is being most angelic. Just when she is bearing her cross most meekly.

Oh, woman out of bounds is a devil. But it is man's fault. Woman never *asked,* in the first place, to be cast out of her bit of an Eden of belief and trust. It is man's business to bear the responsibility of belief. If he becomes a spiritual fornicator and liar, like . . . Arthur Dimmesdale, how *can* a woman believe in him? Belief doesn't go by choice. And if a woman doesn't believe in a *man,* she believes, essentially, in nothing. She becomes, willy-nilly, a devil.

A devil she is, and a devil she will be. And most men will succumb to her devilishness.

Hester Prynne was a devil. Even when she was so meekly going round as a sick-nurse. Poor Hester. Part of her wanted to be saved from her own devilishness. And another part wanted to go on and on in devilishness, for revenge. Revenge! REVENGE! It is this that fills the unconscious spirit of woman to-day. Revenge against man, and against the spirit of man, which has betrayed her into unbelief. Even when she is most sweet and a salvationist, she is her most devilish, is woman. . . .

Hester was scared only of one result of her sin: Pearl. Pearl, the scarlet letter incarnate. The little girl. When women bear children, they produce either devils or sons with gods in them. And it is an evolutionary process. The devil in Hester produced a purer devil in Pearl. And the devil in Pearl will produce— she married an Italian Count—a piece of purer devilishness still.

And so from hour to hour we ripe and ripe.

And then from hour to hour we rot and rot.

There was that in the child "which often impelled Hester to ask in bitterness of heart, whether it were for good or ill that the poor little creature had been born at all."

For ill, Hester. But don't worry. Ill is as necessary as good. Malevolence is as necessary as benevolence. If you have brought forth, spawned, a young malevolence, be sure there is a rampant falseness in the world against which this malevolence must be turned. Falseness has to be bitten and bitten, till it is bitten to death. Hence Pearl.

Pearl. Her own mother compares her to the demon of plague, or scarlet fever, in her red dress. But then plague is necessary to destroy a rotten, false humanity.

Pearl, the devilish girl-child, who can be so tender and loving and *understanding,* and then, when she has understood, will give you a hit across the mouth, and turn on you with a grin of sheer diabolic jeering.

Serves you right, you shouldn't be *understood.* That is your vice. You shouldn't want to be loved, and then you'd not get hit across the mouth. Pearl will love you: marvellously. And she'll hit you across the mouth: oh, so neatly. And serves you right.

Pearl is perhaps the most modern child in all literature. . . .

A little demon! But her mother, and the saintly Dimmesdale, had borne her. And Pearl, by the very openness of her perversity, was more straightforward than her parents. She flatly refuses any Heavenly Father, seeing the earthly one such a fraud. And she has the pietistic Dimmesdale on toast, spits right in his eye: in both his eyes.

Poor, brave, tormented little soul, always in a state of recoil, she'll be a devil to men when she grows up. But the men deserve it. If they'll let themselves be "drawn," by her loving understanding, they deserve that she shall slap them across the mouth the moment they *are* drawn. The chickens! Drawn and trussed.

Poor little phenomenon of a modern child, she'll grow up into the devil of a modern woman. The nemesis of weak-kneed modern men, craving to be love-drawn.

The third person in the diabolic trinity, or triangle, of the Scarlet Letter, is Hester's first husband, Roger Chillingworth. He is an old Elizabethan physician with a grey beard and a long-furred coat and a twisted shoulder. Another healer. But something of an alchemist, a magician. He is a magician on the verge of modern science, like Francis Bacon.

Roger Chillingworth is of the old order of intellect, in direct line from the mediaeval Roger Bacon alchemists. He has an old, intellectual belief in the dark sciences, the Hermetic philosophies. He is no Christian, no selfless aspirer. He is not an aspirer. He is the old authoritarian in man. The old male authority. But without passional belief. Only intellectual belief in himself and his male authority. . . .

It is the soul of the pure preacher, that false thing, which they are after. And the crippled physician—this other healer—blackly vengeful in his old, distorted male authority, and the "loving" woman, they bring down the saint between them.

A black and complementary hatred, akin to love, is what Chillingworth feels for the young, saintly parson. And Dimmesdale responds, in a hideous kind of love. Slowly the saint's life is poisoned. But the black old physician smiles, and tries to keep him alive. Dimmesdale goes in for self-torture, self-lashing, lashing his own white, thin, spiritual saviour's body. The dark old Chillingworth listens outside the door and laughs, and prepares another medicine, so that the game can go on longer. And the saint's very soul goes rotten. Which is the supreme triumph. Yet he keeps up appearances still.

The black, vengeful soul of the crippled, masterful male, still dark in his authority: and the white ghastliness of the fallen saint! The two halves of manhood mutually destroying one another.

Dimmesdale has a "coup" in the very end. He gives the whole show away by confessing publicly on the scaffold, and dodging into death, leaving Hester dished, and Roger as it were, doubly cuckolded. It is a neat last revenge. . . .

But the child Pearl will be on in the next act, with her Italian Count and a new brood of vipers. . . .

It is a marvellous allegory. It is to me one of the greatest allegories in all literature, *The Scarlet Letter.* Its marvellous under-meaning! And its perfect· duplicity.

From *Studies in Classic American Literature* (New York: Thomas Seltzer, Inc., 1923), pp.125-28, 130-33, 137-38, 142-47.

F. O. MATTHIESSEN

The Scarlet Letter

WHY HAWTHORNE came nearest to achieving that wholeness [of imaginative composition] in *The Scarlet Letter* may be accounted for in various ways. The grounds on which, according to Trollope, its superiority was 'plain to anyone who had himself been concerned in the writing of novels' were that here Hawthorne had developed his most coherent plot. Its symmetrical design is built around the three scenes on the scaffold of the pillory. There Hester endures her public shaming in the opening chapter. There, midway through the book, the minister, who has been driven almost crazy by his guilt but has lacked the resolution to confess it, ascends one midnight for self-torture, and is joined by Hester, on her way home from watching at a deathbed, and there they are overseen by Chillingworth. There, also, at the end, just after his own knowledge of suffering has endowed his tongue with eloquence in his great election sermon, the exhausted and death-stricken Dimmesdale totters to confess his sin at last to the incredulous and only half-comprehending crowd, and to die in Hester's arms.

Moreover, Hawthorne has also managed here his utmost approach to the inseparability of elements that James insisted on when he said that 'character, in any sense in which we can get at it, is action, and action is plot.' Of his four romances, this one grows most organically out of the interactions between the characters, depends least on the backdrops of scenery that so often impede the action in *The Marble Faun*. Furthermore, his integrity of effect is due in part to the incisive contrasts among the human types he is presenting. The sin of Hester and the minister, a sin of passion not of principle, is not the worst in the world, as they are aware, even in the depths of their misery. She feels that what they did 'had a consecration of its own'; he knows that at least they have never 'violated, in cold blood, the sanctity of a human heart.' They are distinguished from the wronged husband in accordance with the theological doctrine that excessive love for things which should take only a secondary place in the affections, though leading to the sin of lust, is less grave than love distorted, love turned from God and from his creatures, into self-consuming envy and vengeful pride. The courses that these three run are also in natural accord with their characters as worked upon by circumstance. The physician's native power in reading the human soul, when unsupported by any moral sympathies, leaves him open to degradation, step by step, from a man into a fiend. Dimmesdale, in his indecisive waverings, filled as he is with penance but no penitence, remains in touch with reality only in proportion to his anguish. The slower, richer movement of Hester is harder to characterize in a sentence. Even Chillingworth, who had married her as a young girl in the knowledge that she responded with no love for his old and slightly deformed frame, even he, after all that has happened, can still almost pity her 'for the good that has been wasted' in her nature. Her purgatorial course through the book is from desperate recklessness to a strong, placid acceptance of her suffering and retribution.

But beyond any interest in ordering of plot or in lucid discrimination between characters, Hawthorne's imaginative energy seems to have been called out to the full here by the continual correspondences that his theme allowed him to make between external events and inner significances. Once again his version of this transcendental habit took it straight back to the seventeenth century, and made it something more complex than the harmony between sunrise and a young poet's soul. In the realm of natural phenomena, Hawthorne examined the older world's common belief that great events were foreboded by supernatural omens, and remarked how 'it was, indeed, a majestic idea, that the destiny of nations should be revealed, in these awful hieroglyphics, on the cope of heaven.' But when Dimmesdale, in his vigil on the scaffold, beholds an immense dull red letter in the zenith, Hawthorne attributes it solely to his diseased imagination, which sees in everything his own morbid concerns. Hawthorne remarks that the strange light was 'doubtless caused' by a meteor 'bur.ing out to waste'; and yet he also allows the sexton to ask the minister the next morning if he had heard of the portent, which had been interpreted to stand for Angel, since Governor Winthrop had died during the night.

Out of such variety of symbolical reference Hawthorne developed one of his most fertile resources, the device of multiple choice, which James was to carry so much further in his desire to present a sense of the intricacy of any situation for a perceptive being. One main source of Hawthorne's method lay in these remarkable providences, which his imagination felt challenged to search for the amount of emblematic truth that might lie hidden among their superstitions. He spoke at one point in this story of how 'individuals of wiser faith' in the colony, while recognizing God's Providence in human affairs, knew that it 'promotes its purposes without aiming at the stage-effect of what is called miraculous interposition.' But he could not resist experimenting with this dramatic value, and his imagination had become so accustomed to the weirdly lighted world of Cotton Mather that even the fanciful possibilities of the growth of the stigma on Dimmesdale did not strike him as grotesque. But when the minister 'unbreasts' his guilt at last, the literal correspondence of that metaphor to a scarlet letter in his flesh, in strict accord with medieval and Spenserian personifications, is apt to strike us as a mechanical delimitation of what would otherwise have freer symbolical range.

For Hawthorne its value consisted in the variety of explanations to which it gave rise. Some affirmed that the minister had begun a course of self-mortification on the very day on which Hester Prynne had first been compelled to wear her ignominious badge, and had thus inflicted this hideous scar. Others held that Roger Chillingworth, 'being a potent necromancer, had caused it to appear, through the agency of magic and poisonous drugs.' Still others, 'those best able to appreciate the minister's peculiar sensibility, and the wonderful operation of his spirit upon the body,' whispered that 'the awful symbol was the effect of the ever-active tooth of remorse,' gnawing from his inmost heart outward. With that Hawthorne leaves his reader to choose among these theories. He does not literally accept his own allegory, and yet he finds it symbolically valid because of its psychological exactitude. His most telling stroke comes when he adds that certain spectators of the whole scene denied that there was any mark whatever on Dimmesdale's breast. These witnesses were among the most respectable in the community, including his fellow-ministers who were determined to defend his spotless character. These main-tained also that his dying confession was to be taken only in its general significance, that he 'had desired, by yielding up his breath in the arms of that fallen woman, to express to the world how utterly nugatory is the choicest of man's own righteousness.' But for this interpretation, so revelatory of its influential proponents, Hawthorne leaves not one shred of evidence.

It should not be thought that his deeply ingrained habit of apprehending truth through emblems needed any sign of miraculous intervention to set it into action. Another aspect of the intricate correspondences that absorbed him is provided by Pearl. She is worth dissecting as the purest type of Spenserian characterization, which starts with abstract qualities and hunts for their proper embodiment; worth murdering, most modern readers of fiction would hold, since the tedious reiteration of what she stands for betrays Hawthorne at his most barren.

When Hester returned to the prison after standing her time on the scaffold, the infant she had clasped so tightly to her breast suddenly writhed in convul-sions of pain, 'a forcible type, in its little frame, of the moral agony' that its mother had borne throughout the day. As the story advances, Hawthorne sees in this child 'the freedom of a broken law.' In the perverseness of some of her antics, in the heartless mockery that can shine from her bright black eyes, she sometimes seems to her harassed mother almost a witch-baby. But Hester clings to the hope that her girl has capacity for strong affection, which needs only to be awakened by sympathy; and when there is some talk by the authorities of taking the wilful child's rearing into their own hands, Hester also clings to her possession of it as both her torture and happiness, her blessing and retribution, the one thing that has kept her soul alive in its hours of desperation.

Hawthorne's range of intention in this characterization comes out most fully in the scene where Hester and the minister have met in the woods, and are alone for the first time after so many years. Her resolution to save him from Chillingworth's spying, by flight together back to England, now sweeps his undermined spirit before it. In their moment of reunion, the one moment of released passion in the book, the beauty that has been hidden behind the frozen mask of her isolation reasserts itself. She takes off the formal cap that has confined the dark radiance of her hair and lets it stream down on her shoulders; she impulsively unfastens the badge of her shame and throws it to the ground.

At that moment the minister sees Pearl, who has been playing by the brook, returning along the other side of it. Picked out by a beam of sunlight, with some wild flowers in her hair, she reminds Hester of 'one of the fairies, whom we left in our dear old England,' a sad reflection on the rich folklore that had been banished by the Puritans along with the maypoles. But as the two parents stand watching their child for the first time together, the graver thought comes to them that she is 'the living hieroglyphic' of all they have sought to hide, of their inseparably intertwined fate.

As Pearl sees her mother, she stops by a pool, and her reflected image seems to communicate to her something 'of its own shadowy and intangible quality.' Confronted with this double vision, dissevered from her by the brook, Hester feels, 'in some indistinct and tantalizing manner,' suddenly estranged from the child, who now fixes her eyes on her mother's breast. She refuses Hester's bidding to come to her. Instead she points her finger, and stamps her foot, and becomes all at once a little demon of extravagant protest, all of whose wild gestures are redoubled at her feet. Hester understands what the matter is, that the child is outraged by the unaccustomed change in her appearance. So she wearily picks up the letter, which had fallen just short of the brook, and hides her luxuriant hair once more beneath her cap. At that Pearl is mollified and bounds across to them. During the weeks leading up to this scene, she had begun to show an increasing curiosity about the letter, and had tormented her mother with questions. Now she asks whether the minister will walk back with them, hand in hand, to the village, and when he declines, she flings away from his kiss, because he is not 'bold' and 'true.' The question is increasingly raised for the reader, just how much of the situation this strange child understands.

Thus, when the stiff layers of allegory have been peeled away, even Hawthorne's conception of Pearl is seen to be based on exact psychological notation. She suggests something of the terrifying precocity which [Jonathan] Edwards' acute dialectic of the feelings revealed in the children who came under his observation during the emotional strain of the Great Awakening. She suggests, even more directly, James' *What Maisie Knew,* though it is typical of the later writer's refinement of skill and sophistication that he would set himself the complicated problem of having both parents divorced and married again, of making the child the innocent meeting ground for a liaison between the step-parents, and of confining his report on the situation entirely to what could be glimpsed through the child's inscrutable eyes.

The symbolical intricacies of *The Scarlet Letter* open out on every fresh examination of the book, since there is hardly a scene where there are not to be found some subsidiary correspondences like those presented by the stream of separation, which just failed to carry with it the token of Hester's miserable past that she had tried in vain to fling from her. Again, the forest itself, with its straggling path, images to Hester 'the moral wilderness in which she had so long been wandering'; and while describing it Hawthorne may have taken a glance back at Spenser's Wood of Errour. The clue to the success or failure of such analogies seems to consist in the measure of sound doctrine, or of imaginative fitness, or of both, which lies behind them. When they require the first and are without it, the result can be as mawkish as when [in *The Marble Faun*] Kenyon's anxious eyes followed the flight of doves upward from Hilda's deserted window, in the hope that 'he might see her gentle and sweet face shining down upon him, midway towards heaven, as if she had flown thither for a day or two, just to visit her kindred, but had been drawn earthward again by the spell of unacknowledged love.' It is embarrassing even to quote such a sentence, which, however, would undoubtedly have pleased Mrs. Hawthorne, whom her husband sometimes called his 'Dove.' But having made out a case for Pearl, who, judging from other critics, may well be the most unpopular little girl in fiction, it seemed only fair to present Hawthorne at his worst.

His usually firm moral perception is vitiated very rarely by such overtones of the era of *Godey's Lady's Book* and the genteel female. His occasional extreme lapses from imaginative fitness seem even less necessary. It is impossible to see on what basis he could have thought it effective to remark [in *The House of the Seven Gables*] that Judge Pyncheon's excessive warmth of manner, as he walked through the town just before the election for governor, required, 'such, at least, was the rumor about town, an extra passage of the water-carts ... in order to lay the dust occasioned by so much extra sunshine.' There is no lack here of Hawthorne's shrewd observation of the Judge's sinister hypocrisy; and it is conceivable, that if this remark had been phrased as a gibe by some corner-store philosopher, its Yankee wryness might have succeeded. But woven as it is into the sober texture of Hawthorne's exposition, it seems the almost perfect instance of Coleridge's statement that the images of fancy 'have no connexion natural or moral, but are yoked together ... by means of some accidental coincidence.' The way that Hawthorne's intrusive notion robs his narrative of all sustained illusion at this point is the kind of thing James objected to most. James insisted that the creator must regard his creation seriously, that he must respect its life with the strictest detachment, and keep out all traces of his own irrelevant comments on his characters. These convulsive outbreaks of Hawthorne's fancy might be attributed to the fact that he felt such an irresistible compulsion to look for correspondences that he could not check himself even when he turned up bad ones. His lack of a critical audience is again telling at this point, as is his sense of the difficulties he had to overcome if his imagination was to flow freely.

The ideal surroundings that he described for starting his imagination off enter again and again into its most successful products. He reiterated, in a sentence in *The Snow-Image* that Melville marked, his belief that the moon creates, 'like the imaginative power, a beautiful strangeness in familiar objects.' In some of his pale demonstrations of that truth he may seem merely to bear out another remark, which can be turned devastatingly against him, that 'feminine achievements in literature' are so many 'pretty fancies of snow and moonlight.' Yet it is also true that an extraordinary number of his major scenes are played out under these rays. Or rather, the light does not remain a dramatic property, but becomes itself a central actor. Such is the case with the meteoric exhalations that harrow Dimmesdale with the thought that knowledge of his hidden guilt is spread over the whole broad heavens; and an even more dynamic role is played by the rising moon during Judge Pyncheon's night watch, since, as it fingers its way through the windows, it is the only living thing in the room. . . .

In all these scenes Hawthorne draws on every possible contrast between lights and darks; and the way he invariably focuses attention on the thought-burdened faces of his characters justifies the frequent comparison between his kind of scrutiny and Rembrandt's. Moreover, despite his relative ignorance of painting, he deliberately created, throughout his work, sustained landscapes of low-pitched tones to heighten the effects of his foreground. He generally visualized his outdoor scenes in neutral 'gray and russet,' . . . At the very start of *The Scarlet Letter* Hawthorne calls it 'the darkening close of a tale of human frailty and sorrow,' and in nearly every scene the somber values are underscored. For instance, the minister and Hester are made to meet in 'the gray twilight' of the forest; and the single 'flood of sunshine' in the book, which Hawthorne emphasizes by using these words as the title of the chapter, falls first on Hester in her moment of release, and then is shifted, like a spotlight, to the figure of the child at the brook. Calling attention thus to these devices makes them sound more theatrical than they are in their subdued operation; and one of the most subtle effects of the tragedy derives from the way in which the words 'shadowy' and 'shadowlike' are reiterated in the closing pages as a means of building up to the final sentence. This sentence describes how the heraldic device of the letter, which was carved even on Hester's gravestone, might serve—through its dramatic contrast of a sable field with the A, gules—as a motto for the whole legend, 'so somber is it, and relieved only by one ever-glowing point of light gloomier than the shadow.'

From *American Renaissance: Art and Expression in the Age of Emerson and Whitman* (New York: Oxford Univ. Press, 1941), pp. 275-82.

DONALD A. RINGE

Hawthorne's Psychology of the Head and Heart

HAWTHORNE EXPLORES possible solutions to the problem [of life in an evil world] throughout his works, and making use of the head-heart psychology, sees man torn between these two elements in his make-up. . . . To a certain extent, the heart may be equated with nature and the head with art, that is, intellectual activity in philosophy, art, or science. In other words, the head is that quality which raises men above the level of animals. We must not assume that Hawthorne placed his entire faith in either head or heart; rather, both are necessary elements that must be present in every man. Nor can we assume that either is inherently good or bad. Hawthorne often refers to the heart as a foul cavern, and the dangers of too great a reliance on heart alone are exemplified in the character of Hollingsworth in *The Blithedale Romance*. The head, however, is inherently no better. The cold, speculative, intellectual man commits a sin of isolation which must eventually destroy him. Coverdale in *Blithedale* and Holgrave in *The House of the Seven Gables* are good examples. Coverdale's prying interest in other people's hearts almost dehumanizes him, and Holgrave's inward-looking intellectual attitude almost destroys his heart.

One solution to the problem of successful life, then, would seem to lie in a balance between head and heart. Holgrave is saved from his sin by the achievement of just such a balance. His union with Phoebe adds heart, or human sympathy, to the strong quality of head or intellect that he already possesses. The balance is satisfactory, and the young lovers submerge themselves in the great mass of humanity and live happily ever after in blissful anonymity. For some, of course, this solution is not possible. Clifford and Hepzibah have become much too isolated ever to renew the normal lifesaving intercourse with their fellowmen, and men like Ethan Brand and the Man of Adamant turn their backs completely on mankind, and in their isolation their hearts eventually become stone. When the heart becomes completely withered, the intellect, which must necessarily be egocentric, assumes complete control and thereby destroys all possibility of the individual's achieving remorse and insight through human understanding. The Unpardonable Sin is the result of the complete separation of head and heart. It should be apparent, then, that one solution to the problem of life lies in the simple balance of head and heart. Through this balance of intellect and ego with human sympathy and love, men may attain the happiness of Hawthorne's unselfish young lovers.

This, however, is not the only solution to the problem, and for a small number of people the alternative is the most satisfactory one. What kind of world, after all, would one be, made up of Holgraves and Phoebes, of anonymous young couples like that in "The Great Carbuncle"? It would not be the sort of world in which the seeker after truth in science, art, or morals would be satisfied to live. Therefore, Hawthorne seems to say, if one wishes to rise above the common level of humanity, he must divorce himself from men and deliberately court the sin of isolation. Even though he should fail, he can achieve the greatest insight into the human problem in no other way. All of Hawthorne's seekers, his scientists, artists, and moral speculators, are men of this type, and they are his most complex and most interesting characters. . . .

Thus [from "The Artist of the Beautiful"] it can be seen that Hawthorne believed that he who would move in advance of mankind, who would try to cut himself free from actuality in his pursuit of the ideal, be it philosophical or artistic truth, must necessarily incur the penalty of isolation. In the moral sphere, too, it is only the sinner who can rise above the common anonymity of humankind. This idea is given its fullest development in _The Scarlet Letter_, Hawthorne's ripest work.

This romance develops the theme of the effect of evil upon men, and Hawthorne explores the possible solutions to the problem of human life by making use of the psychology of the head and heart. The Puritan society is an evil one—a society which collectively has committed the sins of Ego and Pride. Mistress Hibbins, the town witch, notes the evil that is present, and the egocentric self-satisfaction of the old matrons at the scaffold scene substantiates this fact. If further proof is needed, one may consider the Puritan ministers, whose intellectual development makes them incapable of sitting in honest judgment on a woman's heart.

In this society, Hawthorne places three characters who represent three of several possibilities for action in the evil world. It must be noted that none of the three characters represents the head or heart in complete isolation; rather, all illustrate the two in conflict. This conflict is least apparent in Chillingworth, for he has obviously already developed an overbalance of head before he enters the Puritan community. Already, his unnatural physical form has been molded by his remarkable intelligence, and his dim, bleared eyes distort everything he looks at with his cold, intellectual power.

Yet Chillingworth . . . is a man who had once had heart, and who still retains possibilities for good when he enters the Puritan society. Even his expression is "calm, meditative, and scholar-like." Indeed, he recognizes his sin in wronging Hester—a sin which was after all an understandably human one which arose from a desire for the simple, human bliss open to all mankind. At this point, Roger Chillingworth is still capable of remorse and is still able to rejoin the great heart of mankind. In his desire, however, for a personal revenge, he pries into the secrets of Dimmesdale's heart, and the latent evil in the man possesses him. He pulls at the minister's heart strings and looks into him with curiosity. The sin of the intellect and the ego has developed into what in its effects becomes the Unpardonable Sin, for Chillingworth can feel no remorse.

Chillingworth tells Hester this in so many words when she meets him after the second scaffold scene (Dimmesdale's midnight vigil on the scaffold). Hester shows Chillingworth the way to his salvation if he will only find it in his heart to pardon. Should he be capable of this, good might result to him, and him alone. But Chillingworth's heart is already withered. He rejects the heart; indeed, he cannot do otherwise in his return to the faith of his fathers. After this point, his fate is sealed, and there can be no release for the remorseless physician. He has become the victim of a dominant purpose which has so completely dehumanized him that he cannot exist in a world of men after Dimmesdale's death. Chillingworth, then, is a man who in the beginning of the novel stands in a position superior to that of anyone in the community, a position which he has achieved through isolation and study. When, however, he embarks on his revenge, he becomes, perhaps, representative of the society itself in its worst form, and descends to a moral position below that of the Puritans themselves.

With Hester and Dimmesdale, however, the situation is entirely different, for in them there is present a true head-heart struggle which enables them to achieve insight and rise above the moral level of the community. Each one sins and each is isolated by the sin, but the effects of evil take different paths in each and lead each to a different resolution. The reason for this is that the balance of head and heart is different in each. Hester is pictured throughout the early chapters of the book as a creature of the heart. Her passionate nature is described, and the generosity of her heart is attested by Dimmesdale and by the works of charity that she performs in the community. Dimmesdale, on the other hand, since he is a Puritan minister, must necessarily be a creature of the head. Though of course he has fine spiritual sensibilities, and though the heart is probably the cause of his sin, Hawthorne continually mentions the learning he has brought from Europe, the intellectual discussions between the minister and the doctor, and the union of "two cultivated minds" that arose between the two.

After the first scaffold scene, Hester and Dimmesdale begin to work out their penance in isolation, and in both characters, the isolation takes the same form. Both give themselves over to introspection, which cannot lead to genuine penitence. Hester becomes absorbed with a "morbid meddling of conscience," and continues to focus her attention on self when she feels that none is so guilty as she. Though she is capable of detecting sin in others, still she fights against the recognition which can mean her salvation. Hester's heart, however, cannot be turned completely to head, for she is fortunate in having little Pearl, who, Hawthorne comments, helps Hester keep a reasonable balance.

Dimmesdale, on the other hand, suffers in complete isolation, for the sin is all within him, and his torture is unmitigated by any human love. Thus Dimmesdale becomes suspicious of all mankind and seeks reasons for his keeping silent. Yet it is clear that Dimmesdale's heart has been opened by the sin and that his fall is working for good. He is already a better minister than his colleagues. Some of them have spent "years in acquiring abstruse lore," some have a "shrewd, hard, iron, or granite understanding," others have developed their mental powers through toil over books and patient thought. Dimmesdale is capable of "addressing the whole human brotherhood in the heart's native language." This ability has been acquired through his sin. Thus, though his introspection continues, indeed reaches a peak of intensity as Dimmesdale begins to flog himself and keep vigils, still it is a healthy sign that he is incapable of self-deception.

Dimmesdale is released from this unhealthy state by his meeting with Hester and Pearl in the second scaffold scene. As he takes Pearl by the hand, there comes to him "what seemed a tumultuous rush of new life, other life than his own, pouring like a torrent into his heart, and hurrying through all his veins, as if the mother and the child were communicating their vital warmth to his half-torpid system." The effects of his partial return to human warmth are immediate, for the following day "he preached a discourse which was held to be the richest and most powerful" he had ever given. Dimmesdale's insight, however, is not yet complete. Though his heart has been softened, still his head conflicts with it, for he still dreads public exposure and covers up with a small lie the mystery of the glove found on the scaffold. But the reunion with the chain of humanity has done its work. There is no more bloody scourge, no more fasts and vigils for the young minister.

While the minister is thus gaining heart, Hester, on the other hand, is developing mind. It is true that Hester's works of charity continue to show her almost inexhaustible human tenderness to those who are sick or in trouble. But at the same time, Hester exhibits a marble coldness of impression which shows "that her life had turned, in a great measure, from passion and feeling, to thought." So isolated had she become that "she assumed a freedom of speculation" unknown in the colony. Consequently, her "heart had lost its regular and healthy throb," and she "wandered without a clew in the dark labyrinth of mind." What Hester needed now was the final touch of heart.

This effect is partially achieved in Hester in the second scaffold scene. Her heart is opened to Dimmesdale, and she loses herself in trying to save him. Her interview with Chillingworth on the edge of the forest illustrates this fact. Hester becomes aware of the deep injury she has done the minister in allowing him to live unaware of the evil that is close to him in the form of Chillingworth. In the early misanthropy of her own trouble, she had left the minister to his doom. But "since the night of his vigil," Hawthorne notes, "all her sympathies towards him had been both softened and invigorated."

Thus Hester, through her long struggle in the moral wilderness, and through her isolation from the community, has acquired an intellect which enables her to look at human institutions with a fresh point of view. She has become strong, and though she has perhaps learned many things amiss, still her great heart remains. It is the heart that tempts her to plan to run away with Dimmesdale, to try to retrieve what human happiness she can from the cold isolation of her life. But one who has gone as far afield as Hester cannot return. Her sin, her penance and remorse, and the insight she has acquired will not permit her to sink again into anonymity. The price of her new intelligence of both head and heart is isolation, ... Perhaps she tries to return to the common level of life when she leaves the colony with little Pearl. She who has insight into life, however, cannot live so unreal an existence and must return to the reality of her Puritan home. People come to her for help, and the symbol on her breast becomes transfigured. Through her sin, Hester rises to a greater height than she could ever have attained without her fall, remorse, and long penance. She no longer makes the mistake of believing egotistically that she could be the prophetess of a new relation between men and women. She understands her own sin and shame, and lives a selfless life which concerns itself not at all with personal profit and enjoyment. Her service becomes her victory, and she learns with Owen Warland [in "The Artist of the Beautiful"] "that the reward of all high performance must be sought within itself, or sought in vain."

A similar effect of the redemptive value of evil can be noted in Dimmesdale. We have already seen that after the second scaffold scene, Dimmesdale's heart has been softened. His meeting with Hester in the forest works a similar effect in him. Here in the moral wilderness with his partner in sin, he can at last be true; he can turn completely out of himself and forget all his selfish fears. The union of the two hearts is effected as they sit hand in hand. Dimmesdale has heretofore watched with morbid zeal each breath of emotion that he experienced, each thought that he had; his mind had been "darkened and confused by the very remorse which harrowed it." Now at last there appears, however, "a glimpse of human affection and sympathy, a new life, and a true one, in exchange for the heavy doom which he was now expiating." Dimmesdale, then, attempts to escape into the great heart of humanity and lose himself in anonymity. It is impossible for him to do so, however, for as a result of the sin he has become so isolated from humankind that he cannot return.

Yet his attempt to escape brings him good results, for as Hawthorne notes: "Tempted by a dream of happiness, he had yielded himself, with deliberate choice, as he had never done before, to what he knew was deadly sin." The influence of the sin looses a deadly poison through his whole system, and he is tempted and frightened by doubts and a gratuitous desire for evil. This idea is objectified as he leaves the forest in his encounters with the deacon, the maiden, the sailor, and others. Dimmesdale has fallen again, has recreated his sin, but this time the fall has a beneficent effect, for Dimmesdale fully recognizes for the first time "his sympathy and fellowship with wicked mortals, and the world of perverted spirits." The old egocentric self is gone, and he walks out of the forest a new man, "a wiser one; with a knowledge of hidden mysteries which the simplicity of the former never could have reached." "A bitter kind of knowledge that!" Hawthorne comments, but it is the supreme knowledge, the recognition of evil which not only isolates the individual, but also raises him above the ordinary level of men.

Just as the second scaffold scene enabled the minister to achieve reunion with men and thereby caused him to deliver a fine sermon, so also does the recognition of the common bond after the forest scene produce a like result. But here, since the minister has now achieved the deepest insight, his sermon is much more effective. Dimmesdale writes the Election Sermon immediately after he returns from the forest. The composition in this instance is controlled not by the head but the heart, for "he wrote with such an impulsive flow of thought and emotion, that he fancied himself inspired." The effect on the listeners, too, is not one which can be grasped through the use of the head. Hawthorne does not give us a word of the sermon, rather purposefully refrains from doing so. Dimmesdale is not instructing, not preaching, not warning. He is expressing his common bond with men, and the only way Hawthorne can express this is through treating the sermon as a piece of music, the art form which is most divorced from intellect, and which has perhaps the purest emotive values. There is expressed throughout the sermon, the cry of pain—

> the complaint of a human heart, sorrow-laden, perchance guilty, telling its secret, whether of guilt or sorrow, to the great heart of mankind; beseeching its sympathy or forgiveness,—at every moment,—in each accent,—and never in vain! It was this profound and continual undertone that gave the clergyman his most appropriate power.[1]

Dimmesdale's triumph, then, is the supreme one, for through his fall and isolation, and through his remorse, he achieves a recognition, an insight more profound than that of any other character in the book. But Dimmesdale, like all men who achieve a position so high above the common horde of humanity, is doomed to fail. Few of the people in the community understand fully the message his insight qualified him to give. Even many of those who see the mark on his chest misinterpret its significance, and many deny that it existed at all. Thus though Dimmesdale achieves the highest moral triumph that man is capable of, his is not the ideal solution. That solution rests in Hester, who does not achieve true insight until she leaves the colony and loses herself in the mass of men. She learns in time, however, that only in the colony does her reality lie, that the world of men is a meaningless sham. With this insight, she returns, assumes again her stigma, and reminds the people constantly of the omnipresence of sin. It is only in the Hester Prynnes of the world that gradual and perhaps continuing moral progress for man can be hoped for or sought.

It seems obvious to me that Hawthorne intended his characters to be read in this way, that he intended to show that man must fall if he is to rise to heights above the normal level of men. . . .

From "Hawthorne's Psychology of the Head and Heart," *PMLA*, 65 (1950), 120-32.

---

1. It can be argued that when the evil background of the Election Sermon has been considered, the sermon itself is the supreme hypocrisy. We must recognize, however, that this is the only way that the minister can produce his good results. The sermon may be considered, then, the supreme consummation of the artist's gift.

GEORGE PARSONS LATHROP

On *The House of the Seven Gables*

IN "The House of the Seven Gables" Hawthorne attained a connection of parts and a masterly gradation of tones which did not belong, in the same fulness, to "The Scarlet Letter." There is, besides, a larger range of character, in this second work, and a much more nicely detailed and reticulated portrayal of the individuals. Hepzibah is a painting on ivory, yet with all the warmth of a real being. Very noticeable is the delicate veneration and tenderness for her with which the author seems to inspire us, notwithstanding the fact that he has almost nothing definite to say of her except what tends to throw a light ridicule. She is continually contrasted with the exquisite freshness, ready grace, and beauty of Phoebe, and subjected to unfavorable comparisons in the mind of Clifford, whose half-obliterated but still exact aesthetic perception casts silent reproach upon her. Yet, in spite of this, she becomes in a measure endeared to us. In the grace, and agreeableness too, with which Hawthorne manages to surround this ungifted spinster, we find a unit of measure for the beauty with which he has invested the more frightful and tragic elements of the story. It is this triumph of beauty without destroying the unbeautiful, that gives the romance its peculiar artistic virtue. Judge Pyncheon is an almost unqualified discomfort to the reader, yet he is entirely held within bounds by the prevailing charm of the author's style, and by the ingenious manner in which the pleasanter elements of the other characters are applied. At times the strong emphasis given to his evil nature makes one suspect that the villain is too deeply dyed; but the question of equity here involved is one of the most intricate with which novelists have to deal at all. The well-defined opposition between good and bad forces has always been a necessity to man, in myths, religions, and drama. Real life furnishes the most absolute extremes of possession by the angel or the fiend; and Shakespere has not scrupled to use one of these ultimate possibilities in the person of Iago. Yet Hawthorne was too acutely conscious of the downward bent in every heart, to let the Judge's pronounced iniquity stand without giving a glimpse of incipient evil in another quarter. This occurs in the temptation which besets Holgrave, when he finds that he possesses the same mesmeric sway over Phoebe, the latest Pyncheon offshoot, as that which his ancestor Matthew Maule exercised over Alice Pyncheon. The momentary mood which brings before him the absolute power which might be his over this fair girl, opens a whole new vista of wrong, in which the retribution would have been transferred from the shoulders of the Pyncheons to those of the Maules. Had Holgrave yielded then, he might have damned his own posterity, as Colonel Pyncheon had *his*. Thus, even in the hero of the piece, we are made aware of possibilities as malicious and destructive as those hereditary faults grown to such rank maturity in the Judge; and this may be said to offer a middle ground between the side of justice and attractiveness, and the side of injustice and repulsiveness, on which the personages are respectively ranged.

The conception of a misdeed operating through several generations, and righted at last solely by the over-toppling of unrestrained malevolence on the one hand, and on the other by the force of upright character in the wronged family, was a novel one at the time. . . .

As a discovery of native sources of picturesque fiction, this second romance was not less remarkable than the one which preceded it. The theme furnished by the imaginary Pyncheon family ranges from the tragic in the Judge, through the picturesquely pathetic in Clifford, to a grotesque cast of pathos and humor in Hepzibah. Thence we are led to another vein of simple, fun-breeding characterization in Uncle Venner and Ned Higgins. The exquisite perception which draws old Uncle Venner in such wholesome colors, tones him up to just one degree of sunniness above the dubious light in which Hepzibah stands, so that he may soften the contrast of broad humor presented by little Ned Higgins, the "First Customer." I cannot but regret that Hawthorne did not give freer scope to his delicious faculty for the humorous, exemplified in the "Seven Gables." If he had let his genius career as forcibly in this direction as it does in another, when burdened with the black weight of the dead Judge Pyncheon, he might have secured as wide an acceptance for the book as Dickens, with so much more melodrama and so much less art, could gain for less perfect works. Hawthorne's concentration upon the tragic element, and comparative neglect of the other, was in one sense an advantage; but if in the case under discussion he had given more bulk and saliency to the humorous quality, he might also have been more likely to avoid a fault which creeps in, immediately after that marvellous chapter chanted like an unholy requiem over the lifeless Judge. This is the sudden culmination of the passion of Holgrave for Phoebe, just at the moment when he has admitted her to the house where Death and himself were keeping vigil. The revulsion, here, is too violent, and seems to throw a dank and deathly exhalation into the midst of the sweetness which the mutual disclosure of love should have spread around itself. There is need of an enharmonic change, at this point; and it might have been effected, perhaps, by a slower passage from gloom to gladness just here, and a more frequent play of the brighter mood throughout the book. But the tragic predilection seems ultimately to gain the day over the comic, in every great creative mind, and it was so strong with Hawthorne, that instead of giving greater play to humor in later fictions, it curtailed it more and more, from the production of the "Seven Gables" onward.

From *A Study of Hawthorne* (Boston: J. R. Osgood and Co., 1876), pp. 235-38.

an artificial code of behavior that renders him useless to himself and to society. To Hepzibah's statement, Holgrave answers:

> "But I was not born a gentleman; neither have I lived like one . . . so . . . you will hardly expect me to sympathize with sensibilities of this kind; though . . . I have some imperfect comprehension of them. These names of gentleman and lady had a meaning, in the past history of the world, and conferred privileges, desirable or otherwise, on those entitled to bear them. In the present—and still more in the future condition of society—they imply, not privilege, but restriction!"

Holgrave speaks further for social equality in answering Hepzibah's complaint that, since she is a "lady," she cannot become involved in the operation of a common cent-shop:

> "Hitherto, the life-blood has been gradually chilling in your veins as you sat aloof, within your circle of gentility, while the rest of the world was fighting out its battle with one kind of necessity or another. Henceforth, you will at least have the sense of healthy and natural effort for a purpose, and of lending your strength—be it great or small—to the united struggle of mankind."

In chapter iv Phoebe comes to live in Hepzibah's ancient house and to work in the cent-shop. A Pyncheon in name only, she serves as a foil to her traditional surroundings: "The young girl, so fresh, so unconventional, and yet so orderly and obedient to common rules . . . was widely in contrast . . . with everything about her." In chapter v, "May and November," the antithesis of aristocracy and democracy is most explicit in Hepzibah's lament that Phoebe is an excellent shopkeeper, but not a "lady." But "it would be preferable," writes Hawthorne, "to regard Phoebe as the example of feminine grace and availability combined, in a state of society, if there were any such, where ladies did not exist." In direct contrast with Phoebe, Hawthorne pictures Hepzibah, who is a lady but less desirable in every way:

> To find the born and educated lady, on the other hand, we need look no farther than Hepzibah, our forlorn old maid, in her rustling and rusty silks, with her deeply cherished and ridiculous consciousness of long descent. . . . It was a fair parallel between new Plebeianism and old Gentility.

Chapter vi brings together two members of the new democracy, Phoebe and Holgrave, in the traditionally aristocratic Pyncheon garden with its "grass, and foliage, and aristocratic flowers." The deteriorating effect of the social snobbery implicit in an aristocratic way of life is symbolized by the diminutive Pyncheon hens. Like the Pyncheons, the isolated chickens "had degenerated . . . in consequence of too strict a watchfulness" to keep them aloof and pure.

An aristocracy emphasizes the excellence and privileges of a few and leads to a dangerous and unwise withdrawal from the world's "united struggle." Thus the express superiority of a state of social equality represents the main theme of the first six chapters. The center of Part I is Hepzibah, the major symbol of a fallen aristocracy. Within this part, Hawthorne arranges each scene so that there are never more than two characters together—usually one plebeian and one aristocrat.

II

Man's need to participate in the world's "united struggle" becomes more apparent in Part II (chapters vii-xiv) as the isolated characters, Clifford, Hepzibah, and the Judge, are studied in contrast to those who are a part of the human brotherhood. Hepzibah, Clifford, and Judge Pyncheon represent three distinct ways in which man is isolated from his fellows. Hepzibah is isolated through pride in tradition and an aristocratic way of life; Clifford through his extreme love of only the beautiful; and Judge Pyncheon through greed. All three have only a partial view of reality. They cannot see life as it is because they are blinded by their characteristic weaknesses of pride, extreme aesthetic sensibility, and greed.

As Hepzibah is the chief figure of a degraded aristocracy in Part I, Clifford, beginning with his introduction in chapter vii, is the main figure of isolation in Part II. Like Hepzibah (but for a different reason), Clifford has always been outside the realm of reality. He had "nothing to do with sorrow; nothing with strife; nothing with the martyrdom which . . . awaits those who have the heart, and will, and conscience, to fight a battle with the world." Clifford's nature isolates him, for "it seemed Clifford's nature to be a Sybarite." He can have no part in the "united struggle of mankind" for he can accept only the beautiful. He cannot feel even the closeness of kinship and love for Hepzibah that she feels for him, for she does not possess the beauty his nature requires for adoration. "How could he—so yellow as she was, so wrinkled, so sad of mien, with that odd uncouthness of a turban on her head, and that most perverse of scowls contorting her brow,—how could he love to gaze at her?" But "did he owe her no affection for so much as she had silently given? He owed her nothing. A nature like Clifford's can contract no debts of that kind." Rather than a detriment to his well-being, therefore, the long imprisonment may have been the instrument that saved what little affection Clifford is capable of feeling. For, if

> Clifford . . . had enjoyed the means of cultivating his taste to its utmost perfectibility, that subtle attribute might, before his period, have completely eaten out or filed away his affections. Shall we venture to pronounce, therefore, that his long and black calamity may not have had a redeeming drop of mercy at the bottom?

The third major character, Judge Pyncheon, enters the novel in chapter viii. He represents in his generation a long line of avaricious Pyncheons. Like his ancestors, he is afflicted by "the moral diseases which lead to crime" and "are handed down from one generation to another, by a far surer process of transmission than human law has been able to establish in respect to the riches and honors which it seeks to entail upon posterity." To the world Judge Pyncheon seems kindly and philanthropic. Actually, however, he is separated from mankind. In chapter viii he attempts to bestow his affection upon Phoebe in the cent-shop. He offers to kiss her as a symbol of "acknowledged kindred," but Phoebe, "without design, or only with such instinctive design as gives no account of itself to the intellect," draws away and refuses the kiss. Despite the ties of blood between them, she realizes that he is a stranger to her world.

In the first part of chapter viii, the comparison of Judge Pyncheon with his ancestor, the Colonel, indicates the reason for the isolation of both these characters: greed. For, "tradition affirmed that the Puritan had been greedy of wealth; the Judge, too, with all the show of liberal expenditure, was said to be as closefisted as if his grip were of iron." Not only is he selfish with what he already has, but he is ruthless in obtaining more, as is indicated in his first attempted interview with Clifford. This incident establishes the Judge as the villain and reveals the growing conflict between him and his poorer relations, which is the central action of the plot. His "hot fellness of purpose, which annihilated everything but itself," isolates him from mankind. He has upset the necessary equilibrium in life by allowing the head to overcome the dictates of the heart. Like Roger Chillingworth, Ethan Brand, and Rappaccini, Judge Pyncheon follows one major ambition to his doom.

In chapter ix the complex and melancholy Clifford again assumes the central position in the theme of isolation as he is contrasted with the bright little Phoebe. As a consequence of Clifford's partial acceptance of reality, "the world never wanted him." Phoebe's nature, on the other hand,

> was not one of those . . . which are most attracted by what is strange and exceptional in human character. The path which would best have suited her was the well-worn track of ordinary life; the companions in whom she would most have delighted were such as one encounters at every turn.

Possessing a freshness derived from her kinship with humanity, she is the "only representative of womanhood" who is at least partly able to bring Clifford "back into the breathing world." For, Hawthorne explains, "Persons who have wandered, or been expelled, out of the common track of things . . . desire nothing so much as to be led back. They shiver in their loneliness, be it on a mountain-top or in a dungeon."

The pathos involved in Clifford's isolation is evident as he gazes from behind the arched window upon as much of "the great world's movement" as possible. Hawthorne describes the

> pale, gray, childish, aged, melancholy, yet often simply cheerful, and sometimes delicately intelligent aspect of Clifford, peering from behind the faded crimson of the curtain,—watching the monotony of every-day

occurrences with a kind of inconsequential interest and earnestness, and, at every petty throb of his sensibility, turning for sympathy to the eyes of the bright young girl!

In the middle chapter of *The House* (chapter xi) the theme of isolation reaches its peak of intensity in Clifford's actions. As he and Phoebe watch the parade march with all its pomp past the House of the Seven Gables, he realizes his state of isolation from the "one broad mass of existence,—one great life,—one collected body of mankind," and he cannot resist an actual physical attempt to plunge down into the "surging stream of human sympathy."

> He shuddered; he grew pale. . . . At last, with tremulous limbs, he started up, set his foot on the window-sill, and in an instant more would have been in the unguarded balcony. . . . [He was] a wild, haggard figure, his gray locks floating in the wind that waved their banners; a lonely being, estranged from his race . . .

Then Hawthorne clearly describes Clifford's great need to become reunited with the world and hints that this reunion can be accomplished only by death.

> He needed a shock; or perhaps he required to take a deep, deep plunge into the ocean of human life, and to sink down and be covered by its profoundness, and then to emerge, sobered, invigorated, restored to the world and to himself. Perhaps, again, he required nothing less than the great final remedy—death!

In the latter part of chapter xi a second attempt "to renew the broken links of brotherhood" involves Hepzibah, who, like Clifford, is cognizant of her aloofness from mankind. Indeed, she

> yearned to take him by the hand, and go and kneel down, they two together,—both so long separate from the world, and, as she now recognized, scarcely friends with Him above,—to kneel down among the people, and be reconciled to God and man at once.

But as the two pathetic figures attempt to follow Phoebe to church, they realize that they have lived too long in solitude and that there is no returning. "We have no right among human beings," Clifford says, "no right anywhere but in this old house . . . " As they retreat to the dismal mansion, there is a contrast between the free air of the outside world and the heavy atmosphere of their "jail," the house.

The last three chapters of Part II are concerned mainly with Holgrave, with the story he reads to Phoebe, and with Phoebe's departure. In spite of the immaturity of Holgrave's notions about reform, he does possess some wisdom in matters relating to the isolating effect of the past on the present. "It [the past] lies upon the Present like a giant's dead body!" he tells Phoebe.

"In fact, the case is just as if a young giant were compelled to waste all his strength in carrying about the corpse of the old giant, his grandfather, who died a long while ago, and only needs to be decently buried. Just think a moment, and it will startle you to see what slaves we are to bygone times . . . "

The story which Holgrave reads to Phoebe emphasizes the two traits which have brought about Maule's Curse and isolated the Pyncheons: greed and pride. Gervayse Pyncheon upset the balance of head and heart and sacrificed his daughter for the promise of wealth. Gervayse's fate is similar to that of Colonel Pyncheon and, much later, to that of Judge Pyncheon.

Except for the judge, all of the main characters are brought together in chapter xiv as Phoebe leaves the old mansion. The contrast between the hopelessly isolated Clifford and Phoebe as she says good-by to him is striking. Her departure takes him even further into the world of solitude. His parting remark to her is: "Go, now!—I feel lonelier than I did." Phoebe's departure terminates the second structural part of the novel. Holgrave sets the scene for the climax, which comes at the beginning of Part III, when he says to Phoebe before she leaves: "I cannot help fancying that Destiny is arranging its fifth act for a catastrophe." From Judge Pyncheon's attempted interview with Clifford in chapter viii to Holgrave's portentous remarks at the end of Part II, there is a general movement of the plot, a building up of the major conflict between Hepzibah, Clifford, and the Judge, toward the climactic scene, which occurs in chapter xv and ends in the Judge's death. The theme of isolation is thus predominant in Part II, and is stressed by the study of the isolated in contrast to the unisolated. As the narrative progresses, it becomes increasingly evident that the isolated figures cannot become reconciled with the world.

III

From the time when Hepzibah's scowl is contrasted with the Judge's smile in chapter xv to the end of the novel, where the events of the story ostensibly terminate in complete felicity, things are clearly not as they seem. Judge Pyncheon, who casts his shadow over this last part of the novel, is portrayed on two levels: as he appears and as he really is. The very title of chapter xv ("The Scowl and the Smile") hints at Hawthorne's concern with the deceptiveness of outward appearance as typified in Hepzibah and the Judge. The townspeople think Hepzibah's scowl reflects her inward nature. Although she is, in reality, warm and kind, her myopic frown stamps her as sour and bitter. In contrast, the Judge seems benevolent but is really a villain of the first order. To the world, he is

a man of eminent respectability. The church acknowledged it; the state acknowledged it. It was denied by nobody. In all the very extensive sphere of those who knew him . . . there was not an individual—except Hepzi-

bah, and . . . the daguerreotypist . . . who would have dreamed of seriously disputing his claim to a high and honorable place in the world's regard.

He is like a marvelously well-built palace with a "deadly hole under the
pavement" that contains, unseen from the outside, some secret decay. For,
"beneath the show of a marble palace . . . is this man's miserable soul!"

The growing conflict between the avaricious Judge and his relatives in the
House of the Seven Gables reaches a climax in chapter xvi, when the Judge
demands to see Clifford. In his twisted mind he is sure that Clifford knows
the location of a long-lost Pyncheon treasure. The climax of the novel is thus
brought about by the Judge's reliance on false judgment made from appearance.
For, the only gold Clifford has "at his command" is "but shadowy gold," and
is "not the stuff to satisfy Judge Pyncheon!" Appearance then leads to another
misunderstanding. Hepzibah finds the Judge dead, and Clifford urges her to
flee with him from the house. Everything points to the conclusion that Clifford
has murdered the Judge and thus ended the constant threat to his well-being.

In chapter xviii, Hawthorne offers a clue to the chief theme in the section
by the title of the chapter, "Governor Pyncheon." The labels "Governor,"
"Colonel," and "Judge" represent titles which to the world signify integrity
and honor, but which, in the case of the Judge and his ancestors, denote, in
truth, a marked dishonesty. Hawthorne pictures the dead Judge sitting alone
in the House of the Seven Gables while a storm rages outside; and by describing all his scheduled activities for the day in which he dies, reveals the
dichotomy between appearance and reality in the Judge's life.

The last three chapters compose the denouement of the novel, and there is
much explication of plot details in these chapters. The Judge's death is a natural
one of the same type that overcame the Colonel, not murder as it has seemed
to be. The daguerreotypist is shown in his true identity as a descendant of
Matthew Maule. Many other details, such as the location of the missing
document, are explained and the story comes to a close with no questions
unanswered.

In these final chapters a constant undertone reminds us of the contrast
between appearance and reality, both in plot details and in Judge Pyncheon's
life. The morning after the Judge's death, when the summer storm has subsid-
ed, even the ancient House of the Seven Gables appears to be a place with a
pleasant history (chapter xix). "So little faith is due to external appearance, that
there was really an inviting aspect over the venerable edifice, conveying an idea
that its history must be a decorous and happy one . . . " This undertone is
exemplified down through the last chapter of the book in remarks concerning
Judge Pyncheon. In chapter xxi, Hawthorne writes: "Thus Jaffrey Pyncheon's
inward criminality . . . was, indeed, black and damnable; while its mere outward
show and positive commission was the smallest that could possibly consist with
so great a sin."

Thematically the most important, and indeed the most striking, example of
this ironic undertone comes in the ending. Hepzibah, Clifford, Holgrave, and
Phoebe leave the ancient house to live in the Judge's country home with the

intention of having the "patched philosopher," Uncle Venner, join them later. These actions seem to indicate that happiness has at last been achieved by Hepzibah and Clifford, who have inherited the Judge's fortune and are rid of his threat. But the level of the apparent here, as in other places in Part III, is not to be mistaken for the real. A recent criticism maintains that

> the Maule-Pyncheons ride happily away from the House of the Seven Gables to possess the future in a merger of bright fortunes—almost a fairy story ending for Clifford and Hepzibah. . . . It's about as pessimistic as Cinderella. . . . Old Maid Pyncheon closes up her cent shop 'and rides off in her carriage with a couple of hundred thousand. . . . ' [1]

And this is precisely what happens. But to assume that the fortune which Hepzibah and Clifford inherit will mean perfect bliss for them is a failure to understand the fundamental traits of these characters and the main theme of the novel. Hepzibah had been fortunate indeed when she was forced to open a cent-shop, step down from her isolated pedestal of "imaginary rank," and become a part of the "surging stream of human sympathy." The epoch of Hepzibah's contact with the human struggle is short-lived, however. With her inheritance of the Judge's fortune she can step back upon her pedestal of gentility, there to remain isolated and lost.

Clifford, we should remember, is a Sybarite. With the loss of Phoebe, "his only representative of womanhood," to Holgrave, Clifford has passed his greatest happiness. He now has "the means of cultivating his taste to its utmost perfectibility." In the closing pages Hawthorne writes that Clifford has "all the appliances now at command to gratify his instinct for the Beautiful . . . " And the result can only be isolation and an "eating out of his affections." For the three chief characters of the novel, the ending is anything but happy, in spite of appearances. The Judge dies isolated from man and God because of his greed. Hepzibah will again be a "lady," isolated from the "united struggle," and Clifford will no longer be forced to see life as it is; he can now view only the beautiful. Ironically, therefore, Holgrave's remark in chapter xiv that "Destiny is arranging its fifth act for a catastrophe" applies not to the death of Judge Pyncheon, which certainly is no catastrophe, but to the tragedy that is to befall Hepzibah and Clifford upon their inheritance of the Judge's fortune. It is an echo of the statement Hawthorne recorded in his notebooks: "To inherit a great fortune. To inherit a great misfortune."

Structurally, then, *The House* is composed of a series of antitheses with three particular contrasts dominating the book. To these dominant contrasts the work owes its major theme: the necessity of man's close communion with his fellow beings. Primarily because of its basic weakness in plot, *The House* is not Hawthorne's best work. It is, nevertheless, much more than a series of unrelat-

---

ed tales that contribute nothing to the total effect but a kind of "irrelevant whimsicality." Organized under a pervading theme, the seemingly diverse elements of the novel can be said to form a "unified ensemble."

From "Structure and Theme in *The House of the Seven Gables*," *Nineteenth-Century Fiction*, 14 (June 1959), 59-70.

PETER B. MURRAY

Mythopoesis in *The Blithedale Romance*

RECENT STUDIES of *The Blithedale Romance* have demonstrated conclusively the importance of distinguishing the perspective of Miles Coverdale, the first person narrator, from that of Hawthorne. Coverdale thinks of himself as an observer of a drama, as "Chorus in a classic play." He holds himself aloof so that he may the better act as an interpreter of the action of the *Romance*. As he interprets, he reveals himself, and through him we get Hawthorne's vision of the internal conflicts which the artist must suffer.

Coverdale rejects literal realism and colors his story and his characters imaginatively, employing several symbolic patterns which fuse with plot, prefigure action, and metaphorically enrich character and the relationships between characters. The first of these symbolic patterns develops through the perhaps dominant symbol of the veil: at the start of Coverdale's story all is mystery, and, as the action develops, the mysteries at first grow greater and then finally are explained, one by one. The book records Coverdale's effort to learn the secret of the relationships between Priscilla, Zenobia, Hollingsworth, Moodie, and Westervelt. The veils symbolize the human situation, and the unveilings comprise part of the action of the *Romance*.

Coverdale's story and vision are based on many of the same perceptions about life as are the Greek season myths, and he employs the actions, metaphors, and symbols of those myths to give his work its structure, to characterize his people, and to describe human relationships. Coverdale, however, has not merely reformulated old myth; he creates a new myth relating man to nature and to the deity and dramatizing the essential mystery which surrounds each man in life and in death. Demonstration of the symbolic and structural aspects of the *Romance* through which Coverdale's ideas on human interdependence and on human perfectibility as related to mortality are expressed will help to make clear the coherence of the work as a whole.

Even Coverdale's more abstract statements about human perfectibility are usually made in terms of the significance of decay in Nature and of the passing of the seasons. Thus when Coverdale recovers from his illness, he says "it was like death. And, as with death, too, it was good to have gone through it," for otherwise he had been unable to fling aside his old flesh like an "unseasonable garment; and, after shivering a little while," to re-clothe himself "much more satisfactorily than in my previous suit."

As the summer passes, the people at Blithedale regard their life there hopefully, "as if the soil beneath our feet had not been fathom-deep with the dust of deluded generations, on every one of which, as on ourselves, the world had imposed itself as a hitherto unwedded bride." And when Coverdale says that "I shall never feel as if this were a real, practical, as well as poetical system of human life, until somebody has sanctified it by death," Hollingsworth correctly detects a "heathen" strain in his thinking.

Later, when Priscilla says she hopes "there might never be any change, but one summer follow another, and all just like this," Coverdale promptly rejoins, "No summer ever came back, and no two summers ever were alike. . . . Times change, and people change; and if our hearts do not change as readily, so much the worse for us."

At the crucial moment when he flees from the playful autumn masqueraders at Blithedale and is about to come upon Zenobia, Hollingsworth, and Priscilla at Eliot's Pulpit just after Hollingsworth has broken with Zenobia, Coverdale symbolically stumbles over a pile of firewood which has decayed "from autumn to autumn" until only a "green mound" remains, and he thinks of the long-dead woodman returning and trying to light a fire with it. As a result of the scene which follows, Zenobia kills herself, and at the conclusion of the *Romance* Coverdale writes:

> But, all this while, we have been standing by Zenobia's grave. I have never since beheld it, but make no question that the grass grew all the better, on that little parallelogram of pasture-land, for the decay of the beautiful woman who slept beneath. How Nature seems to love us! And how readily, nevertheless, without a sigh or a complaint, she converts us to a meaner purpose, when her highest one—that of a conscious intellectual life and sensibility—has been untimely balked! While Zenobia lived, Nature was proud of her, and directed all eyes upon that radiant presence, as her fairest handiwork. Zenobia perished. Will not Nature shed a tear? Ah, no!—she adopts the calamity at once into her system, and is just as well pleased, for aught we can see, with the tuft of ranker vegetation that grew out of Zenobia's heart, as with all the beauty which has bequeathed us no earthly representative except in this crop of weeds. It is because the spirit is inestimable that the lifeless body is so little valued.

At the beginning of the next chapter, Coverdale describes how, in the years that have "darkened" around him since, he has thought of their high hopes "in that first summer" for the establishment of a new order, and he goes on to describe the sad decay of Blithedale over the years into Fourierism and then death: "Where once we toiled with our whole hopeful hearts, the town-paupers, aged, nerveless, and disconsolate, creep sluggishly afield."

The passive and pleasant melancholy of Coverdale's integration in figure of the seasons, natural decay, human mortality, and human perfectibility is not shared by the others; Hollingsworth and Zenobia have, of course, strikingly individual ideas about human perfectibility; Priscilla thinks time can pass without change; and Westervelt can say of Zenobia after her death, with unconscious irony, that "she had life's summer all before her."

As in many of these passages the seasons figure forth Coverdale's ideas, so also in the dramatic action of the *Romance* the seasons are organically related to the destinies of the characters and their relationships to one another. The action of the *Romance* begins with the coming of spring and ends with autumn. Coverdale hikes to Blithedale on a mid-April day which, though it ends in a foreshadowing blizzard, was mild and even balmy in the forenoon. That night Hollingsworth brings Priscilla to Blithedale. Priscilla is described in terms which connect her with the myth of Persephone, the Queen of the Underworld who returns to the earth each spring, as being of a wan hue, indicating "seclusion from the sun and free atmosphere, like a flower shrub that had done its best to blossom in too scanty light." She is sent by "Providence" to be "the first-fruits of the world," who will "begin to look like a creature of this world" if properly cared for. Often in the early chapters Priscilla is referred to as having been closed up somewhere, or as a plant which had been growing in the shade.

In a belated May Day ritual of spring, Zenobia and Priscilla gather flowers together, and Zenobia decks Priscilla out in blossoms. Priscilla is then described as "the very picture of the New England spring," and Zenobia says, "The best type of her is one of those anemones," a flower connected with the theme of natural mortality in Greek myth. And as time passed, Priscilla "still kept budding and blossoming" as "Nature [was] shaping out a woman before our very eyes."

The season-based structure of the *Romance* continues through Coverdale's retreat from the "sunburnt and arid aspect of our woods and pastures, beneath the August sky" and from the fiery ire of Hollingsworth immediately following their open break, the major crisis in the *Romance*. The midsummer crisis divides the book exactly in half; the first half is dominated by spring, the second half by autumn.

The symbolism and the structure, based upon the seasons, reach their climax as the catastrophe approaches. In Chapter XII Coverdale had described his forest retreat and anticipated the "surprise of the Community, when, like an allegorical figure of rich October, I should make my appearance, with shoulders bent beneath the burden of ripe grapes, and some of the crushed ones crimsoning my brow as with a blood-stain."

When Coverdale returns to Blithedale from town on a "breezy September forenoon," the ripe breath of autumn is in the air, which is like "ethereal wine." When in town, Coverdale had thought of the disaster he believed impended as an atonement for evil. Earlier he had remarked that someone would have to sanctify by death their way of life. Now, possessed by the mythic significance of harvest, Coverdale has a presentiment that evil is coming, just when he feels closest to the red clay of the farm where he had earned his bread and eaten it—the farm that was his home and might be his grave: "I could have knelt down, and have laid my breast against that soil." When he climbs into his forest retreat, he finds the grapes ripe and longs for their wine to stimulate "bacchanalian ecstasies." He then comes on the Blithedale folk "full of jollity [like] . . . Comus and his crew . . . holding revels."

Then, when Coverdale finds Zenobia, Hollingsworth, and Priscilla at Eliot's

Pulpit, Zenobia has already been tried and condemned, and, dressed as the queen of the festival with a leafy crown, she awaits her fate. Her suicide follows soon after and the summer at Blithedale is at an end. As the queen of the festival was sacrificed in other times, here Zenobia atones for evil and sanctifies the earth of Blithedale through her death.

And so the *Romance* begins with the coming of Priscilla and spring to Blithedale, reaches its mid-point and major crisis in searing mid-August, and concludes with the coming of autumn and decay. The mythic symbolism of the seasons divides the *Romance* into two balanced parts: spring and early summer in which life and relationships develop and seem to approach fruitfulness, and mid-summer and autumn with their paradoxically inseparable ripeness and decay. At the middle of the book the people are split apart, not to be reunited until the final crisis. In each half of the book there is a journey to Blithedale described, a symbolically important story within the story, a seasonal ritual, a rescue of Priscilla by Hollingsworth, and a climactic scene at Eliot's Pulpit. Significantly, one half begins with the coming of Priscilla to Blithedale, and the other half ends with the departure of Zenobia from life.

At the beginning of the *Romance* and through most of it, Priscilla, and not Zenobia, seems likely to be "sacrificed" at the end. It is Priscilla who is weak and sickly, and it is Zenobia who seems to be loved by Hollingsworth, a fact which makes Priscilla droop. This leads to an examination of the very important flower and vine symbols relating Zenobia to Priscilla and Priscilla to nearly everyone else. The complex symbolic texture here suggests that we are dealing with a myth which reflects the duality of deity and of human nature: in many ways the action and the symbols suggest that Zenobia and Priscilla are partial people, two aspects of the feminine personality.

Zenobia is described as always wearing an exotic flower in her hair, which Coverdale says is more indicative of her proud character than a great diamond would be. Coverdale decides that Zenobia's nature is suited to spreading fresh flowers and reviving faded ones. This is just before Priscilla, the pale flower, joins the group at Blithedale to be revived by Zenobia, sometimes symbolized as a rosy flower. Throughout the book Coverdale reminds us of the exotic flower in Zenobia's hair, which toward the end of the book is symbolically replaced by an artificial imitation.

Several passages from widely separated points in the *Romance* should now be brought together to illuminate what is to follow. First of all, Coverdale, during his sickness shortly after his arrival at Blithedale, bursts out that "Zenobia is an enchantress! . . . She is a sister of the Veiled Lady. That flower in her hair is a talisman. If you were to snatch it away, she would vanish, or be transformed into something else," which partially explicates the symbol. Once, when Zenobia saw that her ornamental flower had drooped, "she flung it on the floor." This gesture of flower-flinging relates the flower symbol to both Zenobia and Priscilla, for though Zenobia is perpetually in the act of flinging away Priscilla as a flower, it is herself she finally flings into the river after giving her talisman to Coverdale for Priscilla. Referring to Priscilla, Westervelt tells Zenobia to "fling the girl off." Shortly afterward, at the conclusion of the first scene at Eliot's Pulpit, when Zenobia subtly expresses her love for Hollingsworth, she is tremulous, like her flower, and Priscilla immediately and mysteriously (for her back is to the action) droops. To Coverdale, Priscilla then appeared to be "carelessly let fall, like a flower which they had done with." And again, at the end of Moodie's tale, Coverdale writes that on that very evening "Priscilla—poor, pallid flower!—was either snatched from Zenobia's hand, or flung wilfully away." It is deeply ironic that when all is lost to her, Zenobia should remark that Hollingsworth "has flung away what would have served him better than the poor, pale flower he kept."

The daily death of her exotic flower symbolizes Zenobia's ultimate fate, as Coverdale so clearly sees: each day is for the talismanic flower what the summer is for Zenobia. And Priscilla, the pale flower, is related to Zenobia through the flower symbols: as the fortunes of Zenobia rise, Priscilla seems to droop, and the ambiguity of reference of the flower leaves us uncertain which of them the final catastrophe will befall.

The importance of the vine as a symbol lies not alone in its connection with the festival of autumn. As Moodie tells Coverdale his story, he speaks of how he described the beautiful Zenobia to Priscilla, and how "Priscilla's love grew, and tended upward, and twined itself perseveringly around this unseen sister; as a grape-vine might strive to clamber out of a gloomy hollow among the rocks, and embrace a young tree standing in the sunny warmth above." When Coverdale wants to gain perspective on the Blithedale drama and pierce to the heart of the mystery, he retreats to his "hermitage, in the heart of the white-pine tree." When he first describes this "vine encircled heart of the tall pine," he writes:

> It was a kind of leafy cave, high upward into the air, among the midmost branches of a white-pine tree. A wild grape-vine, of unusual size and luxuriance, had twined and twisted itself up into the tree, and, after wreathing the entanglement of its tendrils almost around every bough, had caught hold of three or four neighboring trees, and married the whole clump with a perfectly inextricable knot of polygamy.... A hollow chamber of rare seclusion had been formed by the decay of some of the pine branches, which the vine had lovingly strangled with its embrace, burying them from the light of day in an aerial sepulchre of its own leaves.

The intense vitality of Coverdale's symbolism is nowhere more evident; we see, for example, how Priscilla affects her hosts—Coverdale is soon to think of her as a "gentle parasite" to Hollingsworth as well as to Zenobia—and how Coverdale in his hermitage virtually sits in the heart of the mystery of his friends, and, applying the figure again, in his own heart. The symbolic terms interact even further as Coverdale tells us this hermitage symbolized his individuality, and that he sat there owl-like, able, like the owl deity Pallas Athene, to see all "those sublunary matters in which lay a lore as infinite as that of the planets." From his hermitage Coverdale hears Zenobia say that Priscilla "clung to me from the first," and a few lines later add ambiguously, with potential reference to both Priscilla and Westervelt, "With what kind of a being am I linked? . . . If my creator cares aught for my soul, let him release me from this miserable bond! . . . It will strangle me, at last!"

The flower dies, and the vine lives on; each is subject to the seasons, but whereas the parasitic choker only *sleeps* in winter, the flower must return to earth. The vine, though a weak parasite as it chokes, may bind sunlit trees together, even against their will, and may, after throttling them, lash them together in an upright position, preserving a semblance of life in them through its own green leaves and crimson-staining fruit.

In addition to the images already mentioned which indicate the cold darkness from which Priscilla comes to Blithedale, there are other passages which reveal how, Persephone-like, she comes from captivity in the household of a king of the underworld. Moodie tells Coverdale that the young Priscilla was thought of as a "ghost-child" lacking "earthly substance" and so subject to Westervelt, who is characterized in part as follows: "The boundaries of his power were defined by the verge of the pit of Tartarus on the one hand, and the third sphere of the celestial world on the other." Westervelt was "perhaps a mechanical contrivance, in which a demon walked about." Coverdale rarely saw Westervelt that he did not remark the demonic and unreal quality of the man. This interpretation of Westervelt is consistent with Coverdale's perception of his character as expressed in other terms, for his "cold scepticism smothers . . . our spiritual aspirations," and he is "miserably incomplete on the emotional side, with hardly any sensibilities. . . . No passion, save of the senses; no holy tenderness." And climactically, when Zenobia is buried, Westervelt is the first to throw a clod of dirt into the open grave, symbolizing his claim on her as the sacrifice, the new prisoner of the underworld. It is then that Coverdale thinks, "Heaven deal with Westervelt according to his nature and deserts!—that is to say, annihilate him. He was altogether earthy, worldly, made for time and its gross objects, and incapable . . . of so much as one spiritual idea."

Priscilla's life as the Veiled Lady with Westervelt is described in terms which emphasize its deathly aspects. Her veil "was supposed to insulate her from the material world, from time and space, and to endow her with many of the privileges of a disembodied spirit." In her legend, Zenobia says that Priscilla's life as the Veiled Lady lacked reality, and hesitates even to call it life.

But if Westervelt suggests the demonic and death-bearing aspect of deity, Hollingsworth suggests the Messianic and creative. His tenderness during Coverdale's illness reminds Coverdale of "God's own love." But Hollingsworth has channeled all his love into the "spectral monster" which is his philanthropic theory. All his relationships with others he forces to "minister, in some way, to the terrible egotism he mistook for an angel of God." Coverdale thinks of Zenobia and Priscilla as the "disciples" of Hollingsworth. Hollingsworth is one of those who act as "high-priest" to make "sacrifices" to a "false deity" which "is but a spectrum of the priest himself." Like Jesus, Hollingsworth says "be with me . . . or be against me! there is no third choice for you." At Eliot's Pulpit

Hollingsworth is first the passionate preacher and later the terrible judge who condemns Zenobia.

As Hollingsworth functions in Coverdale's myth as a Messianic judge who presides over the sacrifice of Zenobia, so he is also figured forth as Vulcan or Hephaistos, the god of the forge who creates living works of art, artificial human beings whom he enslaves. When Hollingsworth first joins the group at Blithedale, Coverdale describes him as a former blacksmith with features of iron. Later Hollingsworth says of himself, "I have always been in earnest. . . . I have hammered thought out of iron, after heating the iron in my heart." Through this symbol Hollingsworth is related to Zenobia: "As for Zenobia, there was a glow in her cheeks that made me think of Pandora, fresh from Vulcan's workshop, and full of the celestial warmth by dint of which he had tempered and moulded her." The transformation of Zenobia into a work of art through the agency of Hollingsworth is not completed until much later, however, when Zenobia returns to town, driven by her desire to have Hollingsworth all for herself, and arranges with Westervelt to deliver Priscilla back into bondage as the Veiled Lady. Zenobia then replaces the living flower in her hair with a jewelled one which imparted "the last touch that transformed Zenobia into a work of art." The motif is tragically completed when Zenobia ironically becomes "the marble image of a death-agony."

There is irony in this final description of Zenobia partly in the cold contrast it affords with the fire images which have been used by Coverdale to suggest the warmth of her character. She and Hollingsworth are both characterized through images suggesting that they are sources of heat and light, just as Priscilla and Westervelt are described as cold and dull.

The situation in the *Romance* also suggests a connection between Priscilla and Pandora, and the Pandora myth thus serves as another pattern of images linking Zenobia and Priscilla. Zeus, angered that man had been given fire, ordered Hephaistos to make Pandora, a source of trouble for man, and to carry her to where in the distance he could see men sitting about their fire. So in the *Romance* Moodie, the father figure, sends Priscilla with Hollingsworth to the fireside at Blithedale. Coverdale makes much, in his description of his first day at Blithedale, of the importance and significance of the fire in the hearth to the people gathered there and to anyone passing outside. The "outer solitude . . . like another state of existence" looked into "the little sphere of warmth and light." "There is nothing so pleasant and encouraging to a solitary traveller, on a stormy night, as a flood of firelight seen amid the gloom. These ruddy window-panes cannot fail to cheer the hearts of all that look at them. Are they not warm with the beacon-fire which we have kindled for humanity?" A moment later there is a rap at the door and Priscilla, the Pandora-like bringer of trouble, arrives at Blithedale.

As Westervelt and Hollingsworth participate in the myth of the *Romance* as aspects of deity, so the action and the symbols seem to suggest some connection between Zeus-Hades and Moodie. Zeus not only sent Pandora in Hephaistos' company to plague mankind, but he also, as father of Persephone, ordered Hades to release his prisoner so that she could return to earth. Zeus, however, was Aphrodite's father as well as Persephone's. In Moodie's tale, Fauntleroy (Moodie in his bright aspect as father of Zenobia, whose name means "one whose life derives from Zeus") is described as having a home which "might almost be styled a palace; his habits, in the ordinary sense, princely. His whole being seemed to have crystallized itself into an external splendor." If he loved Zenobia, "it was because she shone." But when his gold was gone, this "little lord," "being a mere image, an optical delusion," vanished "into the shadow of the first intervening cloud." He called himself Moodie and "skulked in corners, and crept about in a sort of noonday twilight, making himself gray and misty, at all hours, with his morbid intolerance of sunshine." Thus Fauntleroy-Moodie is a partial dramatization of the ambivalence of deity, having the brightness of Zeus and the darkness of Zeus' brother or shadowed alter-ego, Hades. As Moodie, he moved into the abandoned mansion of a former governor. Here Priscilla was born, and during her childhood never stirred "out of the old governor's dusky house." When Zenobia comes to visit Moodie there, near the end of the *Romance,* he warns her to love Priscilla, and reflects that "in Zenobia I live again! . . . Were I to reappear, my shame would go with me from darkness into daylight. Zenobia has the splendor, and not the shame. Let the world admire her, and be dazzled by her, the brilliant child of my prosperity! It is Fauntleroy that still shines through her!" Moodie is the father of both Zenobia and Priscilla, and each is a natural product of the state in which she was born, Zenobia in a bright, princely palace, Priscilla in the darkness of the former governor's mansion.

The bright and the dark aspects of Fauntleroy-Moodie's character also symbolically connect him with Hollingsworth and Westervelt, respectively. Coverdale fancies the world to be dull and spiritually dead to Westervelt, and he believes it to be so for Moodie, too. At one point Coverdale thinks of Moodie as an "enshrined and invisible idol," a reference which further suggests his connection with Hades, the invisible god, to whom people always sacrificed with averted gaze.

Zenobia, because of her physical, even earthy beauty, because of the relationship to Zeus suggested by her name, and because she is perhaps symbolized by a dove at one point in Coverdale's narrative, may be partially identified with the love goddess, Aphrodite. This indicates that for some of the purposes of the *Romance* the love rivalry of Zenobia and Priscilla for Hollingsworth is comparable to the life-versus-death conflict between Aphrodite and Persephone for Adonis.

One of the results of these partial identifications of characters in the *Romance* with figures in Greek myths is to reveal the way in which they are linked to and contrasted with one another through the duality of Fauntleroy-Moodie: Zenobia and Priscilla as half-sisters through him, and Hollingsworth and Westervelt as sharing with him opposed aspects of his character. Through the myth of the *Romance* Coverdale explores the "enigma of the eternal world," the conflict between creative life and devitalizing death. The tragic fact that in this conflict the warm and vital must give way to the cold and spiritless is dramatized through the seasonal structure of the *Romance,* with its resolution in the autumnal surrender of Zenobia and Hollingsworth; the fiery, consuming loves of Hollingsworth and Zenobia are energetically and even dangerously creative, but they are tamed by decay and death. At the end Westervelt can throw dirt on Zenobia's coffin, and Hollingsworth is only supported in the airy sepulcher of the world by the climbing tendrils of the vine of Priscilla. Fire is hot, exotic flowers are luxuriant, and a summer may be full of life, but autumn and decay are inevitable.

The drama of *The Blithedale Romance* may be viewed as an externalization of an inner conflict. The work, at one level, deals with the artist's dilemma. The divisions in the world and in the deity are projections of the divisions within the creative mind. In order to be creative the artist must probe deeply into life and its secrets, and he may then be accused, as Coverdale is by Zenobia, of "groping for human emotions in the dark corners of the heart." The artist may be aware, as is Coverdale, that through prying into the hearts of others he is in danger of "unhumanizing" his heart. But as poet and chorus he has no choice; he is "impelled . . . to live in other lives, and to endeavor—by generous sympathies, by delicate intuitions, by taking note of things too slight for record, and by bringing my human spirit into manifold accordance with the companions whom God assigned me—to learn the secret which was hidden even from themselves."

Coverdale lifts the veil of man, Nature, and deity, and finds a duality of personality and will in men and gods, and great irony in the manner of Nature's control over humans, who are symbolized both as mortal creatures of earth and, simultaneously, even through the same symbols, as gods.

From "Mythopoesis in *The Blithedale Romance,*" *PMLA*, 75 (1960), 591-96.

DOROTHY WAPLES

Suggestions for Interpreting
The Marble Faun

LUDWIG LEWISOHN [in *Expression in America*, 1932] has called *The Marble Faun* a book "quite without bone or muscle, that is, acceptable intellectual or moral content." He was viewing it as the expression of a private, personal, unnaturally exaggerated sense of guilt in Hawthorne. So viewed, of course the novel is devoid of acceptable content—even of sense.

Now, Mr. Lewisohn tells us that Hawthorne's treatment of sin is different from a normal artist's treatment; and to define the difference, he uses a statement by Thomas Mann. "The difference between Hawthorne and the more normal artist is this," Mr. Lewisohn says, "that the latter dwells upon the process of creative justification of himself and, as Thomas Mann has pointed out, hence of mankind. Out of his need to justify himself he becomes servant and savior of his race and seeks constantly to 'justify the ways of God to man.' Hawthorne, on the contrary, was imprisoned with his feeling of guilt and impelled to state and restate it in tale after tale and romance after romance."

The best part of this passage is its statement that the normal artist conducts a creative justification of mankind. If we test Hawthorne's novel by this demand upon the artist, we may by this very definition find in *The Marble Faun* some bone or muscle, after all, some intellectual or moral content. In the process, we may even discover a connection between the faun and "real psychology" which escaped Henry James. . . .

It has been asked before this whether "nature caught in the snare of guilt" is indeed the subject of *The Marble Faun*. Is not the subject, rather, nature improved by a share of guilt? . . .

Hawthorne is investigating for himself the nature of good and evil. He puts into Miriam's mouth the question whether the murder had not been a blessing in disguise, a means of education whereby the "simple and imperfect nature" of Donatello had been brought to "a point of feeling and intelligence which it could have reached under no other discipline." Kenyon warns her that she is tending towards "unfathomable abysses." But Miriam professes that "there is a pleasure" in such thoughts.

But these thoughts are on the fall of man: "I delight to brood on the verge of this great mystery. . . . The story of the fall of man! Is it not repeated in our romance of Monte Beni?" As the romance of Monte Beni repeats Adam's story, so does the life of Donatello repeat the romance of his ancestor of Monte Beni. It is evident, then, that in this novel Hawthorne is attempting to define the Fall; and presently we are obliged to admit that he is also attempting to "justify the ways of God to man," for Miriam proceeds to ask: "Was that very sin into which Adam precipitated himself . . . the destined means by which . . . we are to attain a higher, brighter, and profounder happiness, than our lost birthright gave? Will not this . . . account for the permitted existence of sin, as no other theory can?" When the sculptor cries out that he cannot follow Miriam in these thoughts, it is not because he thinks they are untrue, but because he feels that they are dangerous. "Ask Hilda," advises Miriam. Kenyon, after some solitary thinking, does ask Hilda the same questions. She shrinks from Kenyon and his dangerous probings; but we have already perceived that Hilda's own soul has been made more capacious and her heart has been opened merely by her bystander's knowledge of the crime. Her well-brought-up conscience simply will not let her admit what Hawthorne has told us about her.

Despite Hilda's shrinkings, Hawthorne, tested by Lewisohn's citation of Mann, seems to qualify as a normal artist, so far as his intentions are concerned. The question would be whether his method is interesting and his conclusion acceptable.

I

Now, there is an indication of deeper than superficial insight in the fact that when they consider the educative power of sin, Miriam feels pleasure; Kenyon, attraction and fear; and Hilda, revulsion. Yet this insight is interesting principally if we consider it from a twentieth-century point of view. Compare Hawthorne with Henry James as a writer of psychological novels, and *The Marble Faun* is nonsense; but compare him with an author who has the ideas of this century, such as Thomas Mann, whom Lewisohn cited against him, and *The Marble Faun* shows both profundity and charm.

One reason for this difference is that since *The Marble Faun* was written Sigmund Freud has given statement and currency to some theories of mental behavior which Hawthorne seems to have objectified in the novel. . . .

To list some topics which interested both Freud and Hawthorne is distinctly not to attempt psychoanalysis of Hawthorne, in any degree whatever;[1] the purpose here is to use a psychologist's statement of some ideas which are discernible in *The Marble Faun* as ideas, treated by a conscious artist, not as unconscious symptoms.

Five such ideas which are stated by Freud are: timelessness as a characteristic of the unconscious; the connection between myth or symbol and the unconscious; repetition-compulsion; the existence of a death instinct; the contest for the soul between life and death. . . .

It may be advantageous in this essay not only to demonstrate the similarity of ideas in Hawthorne's novel to these five concepts but also to illustrate his

1. Lewisohn's remarks, professedly Freudian, on the probability of Hawthorne's having had a sense of guilt with an erotic origin, exhibits the kind of errors laymen make in attempts to psychoanalyze; Freud himself says that a sense of guilt is not erotic in origin but arises from aggressiveness turned inward by self-restraint, and that moral anxiety arises from a conflict of the ego with the super-ego, not with the id. See *New Introductory Lectures on Psycho-Analysis* (London, 1933), pp. 103, 104, 141-143.

modern use of them by comparison with a contemporary novelist [Thomas Mann] who shares them. . . .

II

First, then, to be considered, is Hawthorne's use of timelessness. As Thomas Mann's Hans Castorp learned in a sanatorium that months were of different lengths under different circumstances, Hawthorne learned in Rome what comparative antiquity is. After seeing the "Egyptian obelisks . . . put even the Augustan or Republican antiquities to shame," he set down in his notebook that he remembered "reading in a New York newspaper, an account of one of the public buildings of that city—a relic of 'the olden time,' the writer called it; for it was erected in 1825!" And so when Hawthorne wished to have his reader in "that state of feeling which is experienced oftenest at Rome," this feeling turns out to be "a vague sense of ponderous remembrances; a perception of such weight and density in a bygone life, of which this spot was the centre, that the present moment is pressed down or crowded out, and our individual affairs and interests are but half as real here as elsewhere." For "Side by side with the massiveness of the Roman Past, all matters that we handle or dream of now-a-days look evanescent and visionary alike." Other passages preserve as the enveloping atmosphere of Rome this dream of confused time and even of place, lest we awake from it.

Now, this sense of timeless dream serves a purpose in the novel. It is not mere texture for its own sake. Timelessness is, we are told [by Freud], a trait of the unconscious mind. As an element in the atmosphere of this novel, it is of strong effectiveness in bringing out the significance of such a mythological creature as a faun. The connection between the unconscious mind and myth is, of course, now well known. There are interesting indications that Hawthorne saw a connection between certain symbols which appear frequently in myth and the operations of the unconscious mind.

He not only wrote [in his *Italian Note-Books* of 1858] of a spiritualistic seance that it seemed to be "a sort of dreaming awake" because "the whole material is, from the first, in the dreamer's mind," but said this material was "concealed at various depths below the surface." He thought the exploration of these levels of the mind was important, for he said he could not "sufficiently wonder at the pig-headedness both of metaphysicians and physiologists, in not accepting the phenomena so far as to make them the subject of investigation." . . . These statements are indications that Hawthorne had a general interest in the unconscious.

But Hawthorne shows in *The Marble Faun* an interest in specific symbols. The first page of this novel introduces us to a statue which is the "symbol . . . of the Human Soul, with its choice of Innocence or Evil close at hand," and which is equally a personification of the action of the book which is thus opened. The statue is "the pretty figure of a child, clasping a dove to her bosom, but assaulted by a snake," and Hawthorne recognizes that the symbols here used have been apt ones for two thousand years. Echoes of the symbolism of dove and snake are repeated at intervals as if to keep a pattern. A legend is true, he once wrote [in *Septimius Felton*], "if it is a genuine one that has been adopted into the popular belief, . . . and incrusted over with humanity, by passing from one homely mind to another. Then, such stories get to be true, in a certain sense, and indeed in that sense may be called true throughout, for the very nucleus, the fiction in them, seems to have come out of the heart of man in a way that cannot be imitated by malice aforethought. . . . " Though this was said of the growth of legend, it would serve as a good description of the development of the symbols of mythology, and may be taken as an indication that Hawthorne was aware of the process by which these emerge.

III

The faun concept is the principal element of mythology which connects the timeless Roman atmosphere with the unconscious. The novel is not named for Donatello, but for a marble statue which had set the novelist wondering what the faun's relationship was to man. The novel is his answer to the questions which thus arose. Hawthorne's conclusion was that Praxiteles' sculpture was an expression or symbol of man's delightful escape from his own moral censor: "Perhaps it is the very lack of moral severity, of any high and heroic ingredient in the character of the Faun, that makes it so delightful an object to the human eye and to the frailty of the human heart." Furthermore, the inception of the statue in the sculptor's mind seemed to Hawthorne to be derived, possibly, from a racial memory: "after all, the idea may have been no dream, but rather a poet's reminiscence of a period when man's affinity with nature was more strict, and his fellowship with every living thing more intimate and dear." The faun was "Neither man nor animal, and yet no monster; but a being in whom both races meet on friendly ground! The idea grows coarse as we handle it, and hardens in our grasp. But, if the spectator broods long over the statue, he will be conscious of its spell."

Donatello at first possessed just this charm. Besides this, he had an origin in "the same happy and poetic kindred who dwelt in Arcadia, and . . . enriched the world with dreams, at least, and fables, lovely if unsubstantial, of the Golden Age." He is a personification in fiction as the faun was in marble of one aspect of the mind. Even Kenyon and Hilda seem half aware of a connection between the faun concept and the unconscious. Kenyon is amused and charmed to discover that under Hilda's "little straw hat" "Great Pan is not dead . . . after all!" and "The whole tribe of mythical creatures yet live in the moonlit seclusion of a young girl's fancy. . . . " But on an earlier occasion Hilda has confessed, not without "shrinking a little," that she does not quite like to consider what the source might be of the "nameless charm" which Kenyon felt in a creature "not supernatural, but just on the verge of nature." Hilda, with all her purity, never quite liked to face her own thoughts, and this shrinking may have been shrinking from herself. Hawthorne may have intended Kenyon to be speaking more truly than the sculptor realizes about the habitat of mythical creatures under straw hats.

Since the faun represents only one side of human nature, Hawthorne works out his fable with the help of a second symbolic figure, the spectre of the catacombs. The spectre is not, like the faun, a figure already established in mythology "by passing from one homely mind to another"; but there are indications that he, like the faun, symbolizes in this novel a part of the unconscious mind. The spectre's demon face, which resembles one painted by Guido, brings up queries about its inception similar to those inspired by the marble faun; had Guido "hit ideally upon just this face" by imagining "the utmost of sin and misery," or was it a portrait of a face that had actually haunted the master "into the gloom" of his last years and after the painter's death had lurked in the ancient sepulchres for centuries until "it was Miriam's ill-hap to encounter him"? Is the spectre's archetype, in other words, a product of an individual's imagination, or a summary of racial experience?[2]

In this double symbolism of faun and spectre, *The Marble Faun* is highly comparable to [Mann's] "Death in Venice," where the figures of life, death, and love seem to be projections from the mind of the moribund artist in the story and yet to have objective life as well. Donatello and the spectre similarly seem to move about Rome like visible characters and mortal men, but to be at the same time eternal symbols of two sides of the human soul. These two sides of the soul engage in a struggle for supremacy; and, as in "Death in Venice," they represent the life instinct and the death instinct at war. For an explanation of this contest between life and death, we must turn to Freud's theory of repetition-compulsion.

IV

Briefly, this theory of repetition-compulsion runs thus: Man feels a compulsion to repeat past events which is a stronger principle in him than is the pleasure principle, since it can drive him to repeat painful experiences by recall. This behavior, and also the tendency to torture others or as a substitute to torture himself, gave rise to the hypothesis that there is in man a positive desire for dissolution, a death instinct. Freud connects this death instinct with the repetition-compulsion by the theory that if "life arose out of inanimate matter," since that moment the repetition-compulsion has sought to "re-establish the inorganic state of things." Thus the instinct for death would be the result of life and inseparable from life, even an indication of life. The impulse to self-destruction may be regarded as "the manifestation of a *death instinct,* which can never be absent in any vital process. And now the instincts in which we believe separate themselves into two groups: the erotic instincts, which are always trying to collect living substance into even larger unities, and the death instincts which act against that tendency, and try to bring living matter back into an inorganic condition. The co-operation and opposition of these two

2. There are hints (hardly to be called proofs) that the spectre, like the faun, had his dwelling in the human mind. The chapter title "Subterranean Reminiscences" suggests a mental underworld as well as a physical one. "She has called me forth," says the spectre, as if he might have been kept submerged. The spectre, having been admitted to Miriam's studio, "left his features . . . in many of her sketches." Of certain gloomy paintings repellent to Donatello and evidently done under the spectre's influence, Miriam said: "They are ugly phantoms that stole out of my mind; not things that I created, but things that haunt me."

forces produce the phenomena of life to which death puts an end." This sounds, Freud says himself, like Schopenhauer, but Freud claims a difference: "We do not assert that death is the only aim of life; we do not overlook the presence of life by the side of death. We recognize two fundamental instincts, and ascribe to each of them its own aim."

The use of repetition in connection with timelessness is well illustrated from Thomas Mann's fiction in those passages in which characters, such as Hans Castorp and Joseph, identify themselves with their ancestors. Frequently Mann connects both repetition and loss of the time sense with myth, as in the repetitions of the essential features of the Adonis myth in various guises over and over in *Joseph and His Brothers,* until the throwing into the pit and the descent into monkeyland seem themselves variations of the myth.

So Donatello is connected with repetition and with myth by more than his resemblance to his Dionysian relatives. He repeats not only the appearance and character of those members of his line who bear the marks of the faun; he repeats also the experience of the knight who wooed and lost the fountain nymph, him who stained the spring with blood. And his story repeats (so Miriam says) Adam's Fall.

Repetition occurs also in the career of the faun's antithesis, the spectre of the catacombs: in the rumors of his agelong existence, during which he is said to have prevailed on "any unwary visitor to take him by the hand" and in the gratification of "his fiendish malignity" by perpetrating some mischief, bringing back some old pestilence or "long-buried evil" or "teaching the modern world some decayed and dusty kind of crime."

V

The breath of pestilential death and crime, rising repeatedly from the underground haunts of decay by the willingness of some unwary mortal—this is the spectre's cycle. The animal vitality of Donatello, on the other hand, offers an opposing force. It becomes more and more distinct in the pattern of *The Marble Faun* that the fable of this novel is the struggle between the death instinct represented by the spectre and the life instinct represented by Donatello.

The Borghese Gardens are a world where time works no revenges and where Miriam and Donatello are merged in nymph and faun. . . . Here is the proper setting for myth: "If the ancient Faun were other than the mere creation of old poetry, and could have appeared anywhere, it must have been in such a scene as this." And here we see the life instinct in Donatello contesting for possession of Miriam against the death instinct in the spectre.

When the faunlike youth entered the Gardens, his spirit took on "new elasticity." For Donatello languished in the "stony-hearted streets." He had disliked the excursion into the underworld of catacombs, though the rest of the party, more normal persons, "went joyously down into that vast tomb, and wandered by torchlight through a sort of dream." He could not bear "all that ghastliness which the Gothic mind loves to associate with the idea of death." His ancestors of Monte Beni had "hated the very thought of death" for

generations. They had been a "cheerful race of men in their natural disposition"; so much so that a sinful ancestor had found it needful to order an
alabaster copy of his own skull to be handed down to his posterity to correct
their indulgence in life's enjoyments. Donatello in time has need of that same
skull, but in the Gardens he is purely careless animal vitality.

When Miriam steps into the dreamworld of the Borghese Gardens, and
Donatello drops into the path before her from the tree he has climbed to view
the fairyland, she is uncertain whether he comes from the upper or the lower
world. More than ever, she is impressed by his likeness to the marble faun,
and feels a new affection for him. Fearing the emotion for its very sweetness,
she cries out, "Donatello, how long will this happiness last?" Donatello, who
knows no more of time than of death and can remember his own boyhood only
by his "best effort," answers, "Forever! Forever!"

Yielding to the gaiety of Donatello and the "sweet wilderness," Miriam
herself for a while seemed "born to be sportive forever." The scene then was
"a glimpse far backward into Arcadian life."

But it was only Donatello's charm that created the timeless Arcadia. The
spell presently was broken, and then the Gardens became "only that old tract
of pleasure-ground, close by the people's gate of Rome,—a tract where the
crimes and calamities of ages, the many battles, blood recklessly poured out,
and deaths of myriads, have corrupted all the soil, creating an influence that
makes the air deadly to human beings." For Miriam's model, he of the
catacombs, has brought, as he always does in the novel, the touch of ruin and
of death. No sooner had the "mysterious, dusky, death-scented apparition"
thrown his shadow across the Arcadian sunshine of the Gardens, than all joy
died there. Miriam exchanged her dream of eternal gaiety for a hope of suicide.

When the spectre first appeared in the novel, his shaggy dress gave him a
resemblance to a satyr; but Donatello's instant repugnance disclaims all brotherhood. If he is intended to have any attributes of the satyr, and the shaggy
dress is meant to indicate anything beyond mere realism, it must be the violence
without the sunny carelessness of the wild part-man. In later appearances, the
spectre wears a costume (a monk's habit) more in keeping with his Gothic
connection with the catacombs. As Hilda is compared to a dove, so is he to
a serpent. When he first emerges to our view in the heart of underground
darkness, the actors in the event seem to be surrounded not merely by a place
of death but by death itself; the "great darkness spread all round" a little chapel
where the party stood shuddering, and seemed "like that immenser mystery
which envelopes our little life, and into which friends vanish, one by one." At
such a moment one of the friends, Miriam, does vanish from their circle, and
is discovered with the spectre. The spectre is always obsessed by a sense of guilt,
and seems to carry "the time-stains and earthly soil of a thousand years." If,
as one tale has it, he ever served as Guido's model, it was for a demon's face. . . .

The play of chiaroscuro is so prominent in Hawthorne's work that it has
attracted attention everywhere, not merely as a technique of description, but
as a pattern of joy and sorrow which Hawthorne saw in life. In "The Maypole
of Merry Mount," light and gaiety are associated with classical paganism,

gloom with northern Christianity; a connection which resembles *The Marble Faun*, in which the faun derives from Arcadia and the spectre is twice connected with the word "Gothic," to say nothing of his monastic associations. For normal life, Hawthorne insisted upon the need for both sun and shade, and he went so far as to continue this requirement when sun and shade were life and death themselves.

While Hawthorne was still in Italy and working on *The Marble Faun*, he knew what it was to be attracted to death. This tendency in him has, indeed, been often remarked. *Septimius Felton* decides in favor of the usefulness of death; and the characters in that tale who appear to have the strongest vitality are the ones who are not seeking to prolong life.

So Hawthorne treats Donatello's extreme fear of death as well as the spectre's constant dwelling in the halls of death as unsuitable for a whole and normal person. Miriam was quite aware that death could be regarded as an "unspeakable boon," that darkness of mood was "just as natural as daylight to us people of ordinary mould." She had a curiosity about death which increased even while Donatello's horror of it, after the murder, was growing. Though it was horror which first called upon Miriam to summon her courage and face death by looking at the monk's corpse, she was able, after this, to see majesty in death, even when it was represented in this man than whom there had been "nothing, in his lifetime, viler." (Compare Hans Castorp's interest in death.) Hawthorne says that Miriam was two women in one. She was able to embrace life and yet to face death as the incomplete faun-man could not. Her wisdom lay in this complete embracing of experience, and in this also lay her power to assist Donatello, to draw him from unthinking animal existence, into thoughtful human life.

For Donatello needed a shadow in his sunshine, but he also needed love. Shut away from Miriam in his tower, with the alabaster skull, Donatello learned to think of death, but the thoughts did not return him to life. At the mere anticipation of meeting Miriam in Perugia, some of his old brightness came back to him. When Kenyon sees him in the Campagna rejoined to Miriam, much of his old charm and vitality glow about him without loss of his new manliness. "It is the surest sign of genuine love, that it brings back our early simplicity to the worldliest of us," Kenyon had once said about this love of Miriam and Donatello. Love brings us out from shadow and unreality into life and eternity, Hawthorne wrote [in *The American Notebooks*] of his own love.

It takes both love and death to form the Garden of Eden. Donatello and Miriam in the Borghese Gardens seemed to be a glimpse into "the Golden Age, before mankind was burdened with sin and sorrow, and before pleasure had been darkened with those shadows that bring it into high relief, and make it happiness." Death is needed to make Eden of those gardens; and this "final charm is bestowed by the malaria." So Kenyon wanders in the sorrow-haunted vineyards at Monte Beni like an "adventurer who should find his way to the sight of ancient Eden, and behold its loveliness through the transparency of that gloom which has been brooding over those haunts of innocence ever since the fall. Adam saw it in a brighter sunshine, but never knew the shade of pensive beauty which Eden won from his expulsion."

Now, it is a part of Donatello's insufficiency as a man that he felt nothing of the "dreamlike melancholy" of the Gardens. He not only lacked Miriam's premonition that their hour of joy must die, but when the spectre had already killed it, he cried, "Why should this happy hour end so soon?" And yet, in Hawthorne's description, there had been something in the scene all along that had hinted at mortality. The dance in the Gardens resembled "the sculptured scene on the front and sides of a sarcophagus, where . . . a festive procession mocks the ashes and white bones that are treasured up within. You might take it for a marriage-pageant; but after a while" you see some sad break in the gay movement. "Always some tragic incident is shadowed forth or thrust sidelong into the spectacle; and when once it has caught your eye you can look no more at the festal portions of the scene except with reference to this one slightly suggested doom and sorrow."

Thomas Mann's Settembrini, like Hawthorne, was interested in ancient sarcophagi, and for the same reason; the adornment of the tomb with emblems of life revealed, he said, that "These men knew how to pay homage to death. For death is worthy of homage, as the cradle of life. . . . Severed from life, it becomes a spectre. . . . " When death at length comes perilously near to Hans Castorp in the snow, Hans in a dream solves the riddle by recognizing that it is love that overcomes death's attraction; but he discovers, also, that death is close to the shrine of love and life. The debate in *The Magic Mountain* as to whether life is not "only an infection, a sickening of matter," brings up the question whether the creation of life did not constitute the Fall. This idea is developed more fully in the opening of *Joseph and His Brothers,* where Mann weaves together myths of the origin of life and death. Perhaps the soul was, "like matter, one of the principles laid down from the beginning, and . . . it possessed life but no knowledge." Having no knowledge, it inclined "towards still formless matter, avid to mingle with this and evoke forms upon it." Matter, however, "sluggishly and obstinately preferred to remain in its original formless state." But God, coming to the aid of the soul, created the world, that the soul might engender man; and he also sent "spirit to man in this world," to serve as a reminder to "the human soul imprisoned in matter" that "the creation of the world came about only by reason of its folly in mingling with matter." The spirit's "hoping and striving are directed to the end that the passionate soul . . . will at length . . . strike out of its consciousness the lower world and strive to regain once more that lofty sphere of peace and happiness." Hence, the attraction man feels for death: but "its rôle as . . . grave-digger of the world begins to trouble the spirit in the long run . . . ; while being, in its own mind, sent to dismiss death out of the world, it finds itself regarded . . . as . . . that which brings death into the world." So, Mann says, "It remains controversial which is life and which death."

VI

Now, the transformation of Donatello from the charming but soulless animal into a man by the knowledge of death and love is the fable of *The Marble Faun;* but whereas in the beginning of the book the struggle takes place between the two abstractions of life and of death, the faun and the spectre, with the murder of the spectre this situation undergoes a basic alteration, which is that the struggle between life and death now goes on within Donatello's dawning soul.

This internal struggle of the wretched Donatello is evidently representative of the struggle of the human race. Donatello in his pained retirement at Monte Beni seemed to Kenyon to represent natural man upset by modern civilization. But Hawthorne wrote of the marble faun in terms which would be effective if applied not to one creature but to a certain level of the nature of mankind: the faun had "no principle of virtue" and was "incapable of understanding such"; only his capacity for warm attachment offered a possibility for his education; through the operation of this capacity, however, "the coarser animal part of his nature might eventually be thrown into the background, though never utterly expelled." If the faun and the early Donatello stand for one level of man's mind, Donatello's struggle to become a man has universal meaning; if they do not stand for this, they would seem to have little meaning whatever. Assuming that they do have this meaning, Hawthorne's education of Donatello into "truer and sadder views of life" by his "glimpses of strange and subtle matters in those dark caverns, into which all men must descend," is a universal experience. When Donatello can strike a balance between his new knowledge of death and his natural vivacity, he will be ready for reconciliation with Miriam and will be a man.

When the transformation is completed and the reconciliation takes place, the action of the story is over. There is added in the book, however, a feeble conclusion which betrays by its very sketchiness how little interest its author took in it. This conclusion, indeed, was so far from a conclusion, left for the literal-minded so many questions unanswered, that Hawthorne was obliged to add (complaining) a further set of explanations. By placing his fable in a realistic setting, Hawthorne brought upon himself the difficulty of having to dispose of his Miriam and Donatello in a practical modern external society. He sent them to a prison and a nunnery to avoid crushing them under lives of hidden guilt. From the calf in the Campagna to the unlikely detail of the bleeding of the corpse, details are drawn from Hawthorne's observations, and the surface of the novel is amazingly realistic. Yet the fable itself is "a fanciful story, evolving a thoughtful moral," and the novel is at its best while the fable is progressing.

It is at its best, that is to say, most acceptable as to its moral content, where it is most modern; where faun and spectre are clear in their symbolic opposition, and where in a mysterious timeless realm the instinct for life and the instinct for death repeat the ancient story of the Fall.

From "Suggestions for Interpreting *The Marble Faun*," *American Literature*, 13 (1941), 224-39.

SELECTED BIBLIOGRAPHY

Works

Editions

The American Notebooks by Nathaniel Hawthorne. Ed. Randall Stewart. New Haven, Conn.: Yale Univ. Press, 1932.

The Centenary Edition of the Works of Nathaniel Hawthorne. Ed. William Charvat, Roy Harvey Pearce, Claude M. Simpson, and Matthew J. Bruccoli; Fredson Bowers, textual ed. 5 vols. to date. Columbus: Ohio State Univ. Press, 1963—.

The Complete Works of Nathaniel Hawthorne, with Introductory Notes. The "standard" or Riverside Edition. Ed. George Parsons Lathrop. 12 vols. 1883; rpt. St. Clair Shores, Mich.: Scholarly Press, Inc., 1970(?).

The Complete Writings of Nathaniel Hawthorne. Old Manse Edition. 22 vols. Boston: Houghton, Mifflin, 1900.

The English Notebooks by Nathaniel Hawthorne. Ed. Randall Stewart. 1941; rpt. New York: Russell & Russell, 1962.

Hawthorne as Editor: Selections from His Writings in The American Magazine of Useful and Entertaining Knowledge. Ed. Arlin Turner. Baton Rouge: Louisiana State Univ. Press, 1941.

Hawthorne's Dr. Grimshawe's Secret. Ed. Edward H. Davidson. Cambridge, Mass.: Harvard Univ. Press, 1954.

The Life of Franklin Pierce. 1852; rpt. with foreword by Richard C. Robey. New York: Garrett Press, 1970.

Poems. Ed. Richard Peck. Charlottesville: The Univ. Press of Virginia, 1967.

Selections

In addition to the many reprints of Hawthorne's novels, useful selections include those edited by Newton Arvin (*Hawthorne's Short Stories.* New York: Knopf, 1946); Malcolm Cowley (*The Portable Hawthorne.* Revised edition. New York: Viking, 1969); Hyatt H. Waggoner (*Selected Tales and Sektches.* Rinehart Editions, revised. New York: Holt, Rinehart and Winston, 1970).

Letters

Letters of Nathaniel Hawthorne to William D. Ticknor, 1851-1864. 2 vols. Newark, N.J.: Carteret Book Club, 1910.

Love Letters of Nathaniel Hawthorne, 1839-41 and 1841-63. Chicago: Society of the Dofobs, 1907.

Biography and Criticism

Adams, Richard P. "Hawthorne: The Old Manse Period." *Tulane Studies in English,* 8 (1958), 115-51.

Arvin, Newton. *Hawthorne.* Boston: Little, Brown, 1929.

Askew, Melvin W. "Hawthorne, the Fall, and the Psychology of Maturity." *American Literature,* 34 (1962), 335-43.

Bell, Millicent. *Hawthorne's View of the Artist.* New York: State Univ. of New York, 1962.

Bonham, Sister M. Hilda. "Hawthorne's Symbols *Sotto Voce.*" *College English,* 20 (Jan. 1959), 184-86.

Bridge, Horatio. *Personal Recollections of Nathaniel Hawthorne.* New York: Harper, 1893.

Charney, Maurice. "Hawthorne and the Gothic Style." *New England Quarterly,* 34 (March 1961), 36-49.

Chase, Richard. *The American Novel and Its Tradition.* New York: Doubleday, 1957.

Crews, Frederick C. *The Sins of the Fathers: Hawthorne's Psychological Themes.* New York: Oxford Univ. Press, 1966.

Davidson, Edward H. *Hawthorne's Last Phase.* New Haven, Conn.: Yale Univ. Press, 1949.

Elder, Marjorie J. *Nathaniel Hawthorne: Transcendental Symbolist.* Athens: Ohio Univ. Press, 1969.

Fogle, Richard Harter. *Hawthorne's Imagery: The "Proper Lights and Shadow" in the Major Romances.* Norman: Univ. of Oklahoma Press, 1969.

Griffith, Clark. "Substance and Shadow: Language and Meaning in *The House of the Seven Gables.*" *Modern Philology,* 51 (February 1954), 187-95.

Hawthorne Centenary Issue of *Nineteenth-Century Fiction,* 19 (September 1964).

Hawthorne, Julian. *Nathaniel Hawthorne and His Wife.* 2 vols. Boston: J.R. Osgood, 1884.

Hoeltje, Hubert H. *Inward Sky: The Mind and Heart of Nathaniel Hawthorne.* Durham, N.C.: Duke Univ. Press, 1962.

Hoffman, Daniel G. *Form and Fable in American Fiction.* New York: Oxford Univ. Press, 1961.

Hurley, Paul J. "Young Goodman Brown's 'Heart of Darkness.' " *American Literature,* 37 (1966), 410-19.

Jacobson, Richard J. *Hawthorne's Conception of the Creative Process.* Cambridge, Mass.: Harvard Univ. Press, 1965.

Levin, Harry. *The Power of Blackness: Hawthorne, Poe, Melville.* New York: Knopf, 1958.

Levy, Leo B. "Hawthorne and the Sublime." *American Literature,* 37 (1966), 391-402.

Lewis, R. W. B. *The American Adam: Innocence, Tragedy, and Tradition in the Nineteenth Century.* Chicago: Univ. of Chicago Press, 1955.

Male, Roy R. *Hawthorne's Tragic Vision.* Austin: Univ. of Texas Press, 1957.

Martin, Terence. *Nathaniel Hawthorne.* New York: Twayne Publishers, 1965.

Mathews, James W. "Hawthorne and the Chain of Being." *Modern Language Quarterly,* 18 (1957), 282-94.

Pattison, Joseph C. "Point of View in Hawthorne." *PMLA,* 82 (1967), 363-69.

Pearce, Roy Harvey, ed. *Hawthorne Centenary Essays.* Columbus: Ohio State Univ. Press, 1964.

Schubert, Leland. *Hawthorne the Artist: Fine-Art Devices in Fiction.* Chapel Hill: Univ. of North Carolina Press, 1944.

Smith, Julian. *"The Blithedale Romance*—Hawthorne's New Testament of Failure." *Personalist,* 49 (Autumn 1968), 540-48.

Stanton, Robert. "Dramatic Irony in Hawthorne's Romances." *Modern Language Notes,* 71 (June 1956), 420-26.

Stein, William Bysshe. *Hawthorne's Faust: A Study of the Devil Archetype.* Gainesville: Univ. of Florida Press, 1953.

Stewart, Randall. *Nathaniel Hawthorne: A Biography.* New Haven, Conn.: Yale Univ. Press, 1948.

Turner, Arlin. *Nathaniel Hawthorne: An Introduction and Interpretation.* New York: Barnes and Noble, 1961.

Van Doren, Mark. *Nathaniel Hawthorne: A Critical Biography.* New York: William Sloane, 1949.

Wagenknecht, Edward C. *Nathaniel Hawthorne: Man and Writer.* New York: Oxford Univ. Press, 1961.

Waggoner, Hyatt H. *Hawthorne: A Critical Study.* 1955; rev. Cambridge, Mass.: Harvard Univ. Press, 1963.

Warren, Austin. *Rage for Order.* Chicago: Univ. of Chicago Press, 1948.

Woodberry, George Edward. *Nathaniel Hawthorne.* 1902; rpt. Detroit: Gale Research, 1967.

Young, Philip. "Hawthorne and 100 Years: A Report from the Academy." *Kenyon Review,* 27 (Spring 1965), 215-32.